On Mercy

On Mercy

Malcolm Bull

PRINCETON UNIVERSITY PRESS
PRINCETON AND OXFORD

Requests for permission to reproduce material from this work
   should be sent to permissions@press.princeton.edu

Published by Princeton University Press
41 William Street, Princeton, New Jersey 08540
6 Oxford Street, Woodstock, Oxfordshire OX20 1TR

press.princeton.edu

Library of Congress Control Number: 2018965751
ISBN: 9780691165332

British Library Cataloging-in-Publication Data is available

Editorial: Ben Tate and Charlie Allen
Production Editorial: Leslie Grundfest
Text Design: Pamela Schnitter
Production: Erin Suydam
Publicity: Jodi Price

This book has been composed in Adobe Garamond

Printed on acid-free paper. ∞

Printed in the United States of America

10 9 8 7 6 5 4 3 2 1

For Perry

Contents

Acknowledgements

I am indebted to the late Istvan Hont, who first drew me into the orbit of intellectual history and political theory at Cambridge. I began to think about similar issues and this is the result. The book was started at the Institute for Advanced Study at Princeton, where I benefited from conversations with Bernard Harcourt and others, and finished back at Oxford, where Christ Church provided welcome hospitality. Ben Tate has been an exemplary editor, and I am also grateful to the two anonymous readers for Princeton University Press for their perceptive comments. My greatest debt, as always, is to Jill Foulston.

The book is dedicated to Perry Anderson, who had no hand in its making, but has long been an inspiration.

On Mercy

Introduction

Mercy is a function of the brute facts, though it is the opposite of brutal. Here is one possible example. In *Soldiers of Salamis*, Javier Cercas's novel of the Spanish Civil War, the fascist writer Rafael Sánchez Mazas has escaped from a mass execution and is hiding in a ditch. The Republican soldiers are searching for him, and one of them is standing on the edge of the ditch with his rifle. Someone shouts:

> "Is anyone there?"
> The soldier is looking at him; Sánchez Mazas is looking at the soldier, but his weak eyes don't understand what they see ... the soldier's look doesn't express compassion or hatred, but a kind of secret or unfathomable joy, something verging on cruelty ... [he] calls out loudly without taking his eyes off him:
> "There's nobody over here!"
> Then he turns and walks away.[1]

In that moment, the soldier has the absolute power of life and death over Sánchez Mazas. But he does not shoot him on the spot or call over his comrades to recapture him. He just walks away. His reasons are inscrutable.

Is this an act of mercy? If Sánchez Mazas had whispered 'Have mercy on me, my friend', this would have been the response he was looking for. And if the soldier had heard, his actions would have been enough to indicate that he had understood and heeded the request. Given that this was a military operation, we can be confident that the soldier was disregarding orders by acting as he did. But it would surely have been no less merciful if the soldier had been operating outside any normative framework—if he had been a bandit, or a deserter roaming the countryside with a gun.

In fact, the soldier's action would seem to count as an act of mercy irrespective of his motivation for doing what he did. Even if he lied because he disliked the person asking 'Is anyone there?' or because he was secretly a fascist sympathiser, it would not make any difference. It would be appropriate to say: he acted mercifully because he was a fascist sympathiser, or he acted mercifully because he wanted to mislead his superiors. Just as, had the outcome been different, it would be appropriate to say: he showed no mercy because he was an anarchist sympathiser, or he showed no mercy because he wanted to please his superiors.

What about the soldier's intentions? If he had fired and missed, that would not count (unless he did so deliberately), and if he returned to base and just forgot to report seeing Sánchez Mazas, that would hardly qualify as an act of mercy either. The intention to do less harm must be present, even if its motive is irrelevant. So, if the soldier were thinking, 'I won't shoot him now, because I would rather he die more painfully of cold and starvation', that would count against the idea that this was an act of mercy because the intention is to do *more* harm. But it would make no difference if the soldier thought, 'I won't shoot because I don't care what happens to him either way', rather than 'I won't shoot because he too is a human being and I pity him', because the act itself involves less harm, and indifference to the long-term outcome is not at odds with that.

Yet having acted with merciful intent does not necessarily mean that an act will be merciful. An act of mercy is an action that is both intended to be and turns out to be less harmful than it might have been. So there is no way of knowing whether an act is merciful except by its consequences, which are measured by the harm to individuals. If the soldier had tried to miss but ended up fatally shooting Sánchez Mazas anyway, that would not be an act of mercy. The most that could be said is that the soldier had intended to act mercifully but had not done so. Mercy is defined not by its intended effects but the actual ones.

Three things seem to be involved when we are talking about mercy: the context, which determines the range of possible actions; the intention of the action; and its outcome. This suggests a definition broad enough to encompass a range of culturally and historically specific examples. You act mercifully towards someone if you intentionally and successfully do them less harm than you might, in the sense that doing something else, which you might equally well have done in that situation, would have done greater harm.[2] It is difficult to see how an action that did not fulfil these basic criteria would count as an act of mercy. However, there are many circumstances in which this definition appears too inclusive, given that it is possible to do very great harm that is less than the maximum physically possible.

Some more restrictive definition of 'might equally well have done' is required, but it is important to consider carefully why that is. After all, what, if anything, is the matter with a torturer who says, 'I *was* merciful, I tortured him a bit less severely than I might have done'? One response might be to claim that an action that is in itself wrong cannot be an act of mercy. However, this does not seem to capture what is at issue here. If there are less harmful alternatives, torturing 'a bit less severely' does not seem to count as merciful at all. But with less harmful alternatives excluded, the torturer's unpalatable claim becomes more plausible, even though what he is doing may still be wrong in some absolute sense. To transform mercy into a subset of the set of morally permissible actions is to mistake its frame of reference. A merciful action is one that is less harmful than its alternatives where these alternatives are defined not by their rightness but by their harmfulness, and harm is often wrong.

What makes other courses of action into relevant alternatives, other than their physical possibility? In social contexts, our actions are rarely constrained only by physical limits on our power; they are governed by norms, shared habits, and expectations that, even if not enforced by third parties, guide our mutual interaction. In our thinking, these norms usually take precedence over alternatives that are merely hypothetical. It does not make any difference what the normative framework is; if you do someone more harm than you would normally do in the circumstances, then it is difficult to claim that you have acted mercifully, even if the harm done is far less than it would have been possible for you to have done. So, if the norm is below the maximum level of harm (as is almost always the case), then an act that inflicts harm between the maximum and normal levels cannot be considered merciful, notwithstanding the proximity to the norm and the great distance from the maximum. For example, a judicial sentence that is below the maximum for the offence but above that normally imposed cannot count as merciful, even if it is not in itself all that harsh.

One corollary of this is that the same action—say, execution by beheading—might be considered merciful in one context (as an alternative to hanging, drawing, and quartering) and unmerciful in another (where it represented the maximum available penalty). And if mercy is fully context-dependent, there will be many such anomalies. For example, in some times and places both victors and vanquished would have considered permanent enslavement a merciful alternative to the wholesale massacre of defeated enemies; today, denying them anything less than their full rights under the Geneva Convention will count as unmerciful. Does this imply that we can never tell whether or not an act is merciful from the nature of the act itself? Is the torturer who says, 'I was merciful, I tortured him a bit less severely than I usually do' telling the truth? Or is there some threshold of harm above which no act can be merciful, whatever the circumstances?

Given our usual understanding of what constitutes harm as opposed to pain (namely, that it encompasses long-term capabilities, not merely immediate sensations), there is, at the very least, an elective affinity between mercy and not killing. There may be more and less merciful ways to bring about someone's death, but there has to be a strong presumption that killing is likely to be more harmful to someone than an alternative course of action that does not result in their death. And though it seems possible that there might be a threshold at which life with prolonged pain counts as a fate worse than death, it is still far from clear how we could say with certainty that killing someone without their consent involved doing them less harm than could otherwise have been done, just as it would be difficult to say with certainty that a cruel person was successfully inflicting more harm by torturing someone and letting them live than they would have done by killing them instead. (If mercy is defined by its consequences rather than its motivation, the phrase 'mercy killing' is therefore one that should be used with some caution.)

The fact that mercy inclines against killing, and inclines further than any given norm, is crucial to the argument of this essay. Its central claim is that the world we inhabit (i.e., the social world) is made out of acts of mercy like the one described in *Soldiers of Salamis*. From one perspective, that is obviously true, because otherwise we would all be dead or living with constant violence. What is questionable about the claim is not whether there is any evidence compatible with it, but rather the possible underinterpretation of that evidence. Given that most interactions involve doing or receiving less harm than is possible, to what extent does mercy provide an adequate explanation?

What is it that we are accounting for? At its most basic level it is that it is usually possible to walk down the street unharmed. There are people coming towards you, but none of them tries to attack you. They could, but they don't. And that's not because they think you are carrying a concealed weapon, or even because they can reasonably expect to be arrested and convicted if they do (conviction rates for stranger-to-stranger assault are alarmingly low); it is just because the idea has not occurred to them, or they have decided not to act on it. But the possibility is still there, and, according to some sociologists, we use little rituals just to signal that there's no danger this time. It was not always thus. According to Jared Diamond, in 1931 it would have been 'unthinkable' for anyone to travel from Goroka to Wapenamanda, 107 miles away in New Guinea, without being killed within the first ten miles by an unknown stranger.[3] In some times and places there is more of a gap between the harm that people are capable of doing to each other and the harm they routinely do. We need to know what accounts for this difference, because political theorists tell us that this is what politics is for.

As Hobbes was perhaps the first to state explicitly, peace (i.e., not killing, or being killed) is what politics, as opposed to war, is all about. So it is easy to see that mercy, which by definition will incline against killing even when other principles do not, might have a role in the transition. This essay argues that mercy is a necessary and sufficient condition of politics as opposed to war. This is a novel argument insofar as it claims more for mercy than has ever been claimed before. But it does so largely by default. In particular, it is because less is attributed to the fictive person of the state, and less is claimed for the artificial virtue of justice, that more is assigned to the merciful discretion of individuals. Mercy is a way of describing the brute facts that we are left with when other explanations fall away. The resulting account of the political is radically reductive in that it emphasises the local, the material, and the contingent, and leaves little scope for ideal theory. But it is also one with a wider range of application, eroding division between the social and political, and with it boundaries of nationality, species, and time.

At first glance, this argument may seem inherently implausible. But contemporary political realism gives premodern accounts of mercy renewed relevance. For almost two millennia in Europe, the idea that mercy might constitute a significant portion of what we are looking for from politics was taken for granted. In the *Politica* of 1589, for example, Justus Lipsius identified Justice as the 'Sun' and Clemency as the 'Moon of Government':

> This goddess is lenient and soft; she mitigates and moderates; she sets free the guilty, raises up the fallen, and comes to the rescue of those who ruin themselves. And I cannot describe her otherwise than as a virtue which on the basis of judgement leans away from punishment and revenge, towards mildness. Of all virtues this is the one most proper to man, as it is the most humane.[4]

To demonstrate the point, Lipsius offered numerous examples of clemency in *Monita et exempla politica* (1605), drawn not just from sacred and classical history, but also including more recent figures famed for their magnanimity, such as Louis XII of France and Alfonso I of Naples. Lipsius had himself benefitted from the clemency of the Hapsburg rulers of the Netherlands, but he assumes that mercy is an attribute of successful and benevolent rule whatever the historical context.[5]

The conception of mercy on which Lipsius and other political theorists relied originated with Seneca. In his essay *De clementia*, written for the young emperor Nero, Seneca defines mercy (*clementia*) as 'restraining the mind from vengeance when it has the power to take it, or the leniency of a superior towards an inferior in fixing punishment'.[6] The latter may take the form of lenity in carrying out the punishment, remission of part of the punishment, or even of making the punishment less harsh from the outset. The opposite of mercy is not strictness (*severitas*) but cruelty (*crudelitas*), 'the inclination of the mind toward the side of harshness', and it is this that mercy rejects, rather than strictness itself. Mercy is a unilateral tempering of the power to act cruelly, and, if exercised consistently by the ruler, holds out the prospect of 'a state unstained by blood'.[7]

At the same time that he identifies cruelty as the antonym of mercy, Seneca distinguishes mercy from two concepts that might appear synonymous with it: the 'counterfeit virtues' of pity (*misericordia*) and pardon (*venia*). Pity is 'the sorrow of the mind brought about by the sight of the distress of others' and is to be avoided on the Stoic principle that 'no sorrow befalls the wise man'. Similarly, pardoning is a judgement that may overlap with mercy in terms of its results but involves 'the remission of a deserved punishment', whereas mercy 'declares that those who are let off did not deserve any different treatment'.[8] However, these distinctions are rarely maintained by other writers, and words like *clementia*, *lenitas*, *misericordia*, and *humanitas* are all used to describe acts of mercy without any clear differentiation being made. Seneca tries to steer away from the latter two, but even he is inconsistent in his usage.[9]

Where Seneca had tried to separate clemency from pity and from pardon, Christianity conjoined them. In the New Testament, God's mercy is manifest through compassionately pardoning those who stand justly condemned. And whereas Latin at least allowed a distinction to be made between mercy and pity, the Greek word *eleos* encompasses both. Humankind, though deserving of punishment under the law, is offered salvation through Christ: 'In our natural condition we ... lay under the dreadful judgement of God. But God, rich in mercy, for the great love he bore us, brought us to life'.[10] The church fathers did not necessarily see any discontinuity between the form of mercy offered by the Christian God and a Roman ruler. The saving mercy of God in the incarnation was, Augustine claimed, a form of *popularis clementia*, the mercy toward the people that Julius Caesar was also said to have practised.[11]

This analogy between the mercy of divine and human sovereigns worked both ways. Just as Seneca had encouraged Nero to follow the example of the clemency of the gods to men, in a Christian context, princely mercy could be interpreted as *imitatio Dei*. Mercy is a function of power, so when it is exercised the king aligns himself with God, whose absolute power is also tempered with mercy. This is the idea captured in Portia's famous speech in *The Merchant of Venice*:

> But mercy is above this sceptred sway;
> It is enthroned in the hearts of kings,
> It is an attribute to God himself;
> And earthly power doth then show likest God's
> When mercy seasons justice.[12]

This was not a poetic exaggeration. In late medieval and early modern Europe the royal prerogative of clemency was exercised repeatedly in a variety of contexts to demonstrate that the monarch was merciful and thus merited their power. Its most dramatic manifestation was the general pardon. A general pardon was open to any individual who wanted to purchase it, and though certain crimes were usually excluded, in the sixteenth century those offered at the start of the reign of English monarchs could be exceptionally generous, sometimes including even treason, rebellion, and murder.[13] Such conspicuous gestures confirmed the widely held belief that clemency was at the prince's sole discretion, and the throne itself was 'underpropped with mercy'.[14] The text of Charles II's coronation pardon of 1661 makes the connection explicit. It is said to be offered because the king is 'well pleased with opportunities to abound in acts of Grace and Clemency to His people, from whom He doth also expect Returns of Loyalty and due obedience on their parts'.[15]

The royal prerogative was gradually eroded by Parliament, and with the coronation of George I, the coronation pardon lapsed. Yet at the same time, pardoning in the royal name became entrenched in the everyday practice of the law. It is in this context that the widespread practice of judicial clemency in the eighteenth century should be viewed. Half of those convicted of capital crimes in eighteenth-century England were never executed, and this more diffused clemency performed the same function for the ruling class as a whole that it had previously done for the monarch himself. As Douglas Hay has argued, it was the discretionary application of the criminal law that 'more than any other social institution, made it possible to govern ... without a police force and without a large army'. It maintained both order and deference because 'discretion allowed a prosecutor to terrorize the petty thief and then command his gratitude'.[16]

Montesquieu may have maintained that letters of pardon were 'a great spring of moderate governments', but to many thinkers of the Enlightenment mercy appeared superfluous or even harmful.[17] Hume condemned the medieval practice of 'extorting from the king pardons for the most enormous crimes' as a 'great mischief', and considered moves to restrict the royal pardon to be 'excellent'. According to him, 'all civilized nations' sought 'to remove everything arbitrary and partial' from the discretion of judges, particularly with regard to property, for 'public utility requires that property should be regulated by general inflexible rules'.[18]

The Italian legal theorist Cesare Beccaria agreed. Although he argued for the end of torture and capital punishment, he nevertheless insisted that clemency is needed only when the law is excessively severe, and that 'as punishments become milder, clemency and pardons become less necessary'. Clemency, which had once seemed indispensable to the exercise of sovereignty, should become 'redundant in a perfect administration where punishments are mild and the methods of judgement are regular and expeditious'. Mercy is for lawmakers to determine, not the executors of justice. The laws themselves should be 'inexorable'.[19]

By the end of the eighteenth century, Beccaria's followers were denouncing mercy in even stronger terms. The Neapolitan jurist Gaetano Filangieri called it 'an injustice committed against society ... a manifest vice'.[20] Jeremy Bentham (who picked up the phrase 'greatest happiness of the greatest number' from Beccaria) claimed that 'the power of pardoning ... has cruelty for its cause ... [and] cruelty for its effect'. According to him, 'The government of the passions precedes that of reason'; mercy belongs to an earlier, more primitive age in which, because 'the effect of an offence is only to enrage the sovereign, there is merit in his abstaining from punishing it'.[21]

In retrospect, it is easy to place this rejection of mercy within the context of the wider shift in ethics identified by Albert Hirschman in *The Passions and the Interests*.[22] For a long time, destructive human passions were thought best governed by countervailing ones. Thus, as Spinoza noted, 'to cruelty is opposed mercy (*clementia*) ... a power of the mind, by which a man governs anger and vengeance'.[23] However, in the course of the eighteenth century there was a change. Hume too believed that 'nothing can oppose or retard the impulse of passion but a contrary impulse', but he thought that there was a significant exception: 'There is no passion ... capable of controlling the interested affection, but the very affection itself, by an alteration of its direction'. By 'interested affection' Hume meant the 'avidity ... of acquiring goods and possessions', and it was the equation of interest with economic self-interest that, according to Hirschman, fed the belief that 'Interest Governs the World'.[24]

As Hirschman demonstrates, in the eighteenth century people came to believe that the pursuit of economic self-interest might also be in the public interest, and promote moderation and prosperity in a way that the warlike passions did not. Thus, Hume maintained that it was the conventions arising from the pursuit of economic self-interest that gave rise to the principles of justice, and that its resulting utility provided the justification.[25] This move deprived mercy of an independent rationale: it was no longer required as the specific countervailing passion to cruelty, and it was not itself, as Spinoza acknowledged, one of those powers of the mind 'that relate only to the agent's advantage'.[26]

If mercy had a justification at all, it was that it contributed to public utility. But Beccaria was sure that it did not. Confident that 'commerce has been stimulated by philosophic truths' and that 'we have discovered the true relations between sovereign and subjects and between nation and nation', Beccaria sought to extend economic rationality to the law.[27] People were motivated not by the passions but by rational calculation of self-interest, so the possibility of clemency needed to be removed in order for marginal deterrence to function effectively. In this way, the wise lawmaker 'raises his building on the foundation of self-love' to ensure that 'the interest of all ought to be the product of the interests of each'.[28]

As this suggests, the exclusion of mercy from law and politics was closely linked to the rationalization of political life as a system for maximizing self-interest. Hirschman suggests that the shift from the passions to the interests was an argument for capitalism before its rise. By furnishing new ways of avoiding anger and cruelty, nascent capitalism simultaneously dispensed with the countervailing passion of mercy. Mercy had once been considered a remedy for the cruelties of war, but wars driven by the passions were replaced by what Beccaria called the 'silent war' waged among nations by trade, so now no remedy is needed, for this is 'the most humane sort of war and more worthy of reasonable men'.[29]

If the arguments for capitalism are the same as those against mercy, the consequences are far-reaching. Capitalism offers an account of the way the world is made based on the convergence of our interests rather than the mercy of the powerful. This congruence of self-interest is often called justice, but it is a justice that no longer needs to be tempered by mercy, because its principles are in everyone's interest to begin with. Mercy is therefore excluded as a possible remedy for the workings of capitalism itself. In this essay, I ask whether it is possible to dispense with mercy quite so easily; I then examine the potential consequences of its reintroduction.

1

In *De clementia* Seneca emphasised that mercy presupposes a radical asymmetry between the person who
grants it and the person who receives it. That asymmetry is not necessarily a function of status; mercy is
the prerogative of anyone whom fortune has favoured
in the struggle for power. However, the power to grant
mercy will more consistently be found in a public
than a private context, and 'in rulers it has an especial
comeliness'.[1]

The claim had a history behind it. In the early
Roman republic, mercy had played little role, save
when granted to the vanquished by Roman generals
in foreign wars. During the civil wars, however, it was
self-conciously adopted as an instrument of policy by
Julius Caesar, who offered clemency to his defeated
Roman enemies just as he had earlier done to the
Gauls.[2] This was usually accepted, though for men of
high status it posed a dilemma: to accept mercy was

to acknowledge defeat and subordination. Cato the Younger preferred to commit suicide instead.

This ambivalence is reflected most clearly in the writings of Cicero, who recognised the novelty and importance of Caesar's *clementia* and sought it for those, such as Marcellus, who had fought with Pompey against him. Cicero's praise for Caesar is extravagant, but the argument is an interesting one: mercy justifies the victory that preceded it.

> You had already surpassed all other conquerors in civil wars, in equity, and clemency, but this day ... you appear to have surpassed victory itself, since you have remitted in favour of the conquered those things which victory had put in your power.... You, therefore, deserve to be the only man who is never conquered, since you conquer the conditions and the violent privileges of victory itself.[3]

In other words, because Caesar refuses to take advantage of his victories, he is the one person who deserves always to be victorious; however many victories he has, it is as though he had never had them.

Nevertheless, Cicero (who was eventually forced to accept Caesar's clemency himself) remained conscious that Caesar's mercy was double-edged, an '*insidiosa clementia*'.[4] That there were good grounds for this view can be seen from one of Caesar's own letters, where he unambiguously presents clemency (*lenitas*) as a strategy to achieve the lasting victory that others have been unable to because of their cruelty: 'Let this be our new method of conquering—to fortify ourselves by mercy (*misericordia*) and generosity'.[5] No wonder Cicero eventually presents Caesar's mercy as a ploy designed to reduce Roman citizens to slavery. On the one hand, Caesar's clemency might seem to legitimate his rule; on the other, his usurpation of the republic meant that he was a tyrant, and tyrants are forced to rule through cruelty and fear.[6]

As an ardent republican writing in the closing years of the republic, Cicero is ambivalent about clemency because for him there is ultimately no difference between a king and a tyrant. A century later, Seneca, the imperial tutor, presents the opposite view: there is no such thing as a clement tyrant, because tyranny tempered with mercy is legitimate kingship. The difference between a tyrant and a king lies not in their names but their deeds, and 'it is mercy that makes the distinction between a king and a tyrant as great as it is ... the one uses the arms which he has to fortify good-will, the other to curb great hatred by great fear'.[7]

Although Seneca at this point defends Caesar, his primary example of the merciful prince is Augustus and his clemency toward Cinna, who had been plotting to kill him. In imagining Augustus's internal dialogue about the issue, Seneca presents a novel response to the argument that fear will necessarily undermine any prince who rules by force. Mercy breaks the vicious cycle of tyranny, for, by accepting fear himself, the prince gives no reason for his subjects to fear (or hate) him.[8] In this regard, Augustus was a better advertisement for mercy than Julius Caesar (who was assassinated by someone to whom he had shown clemency), but his policy only inclined to mercy after his rule was established, and Seneca tries to persuade Nero that it is best to be merciful from the start.

According to Seneca, pursuing a policy of mercy not only makes all the difference between monarchy and tyranny; it changes the outcome as well. He does not question the contention that tyranny breeds resentment, but argues that mercy, by transforming tyranny into legitimate kingship, wins the loyalty of the people: 'Mercy, then, makes rulers not only more honoured, but safer, and is at the same time the glory of sovereign power and its surest protection'.[9] For this reason, mercy is not only desirable for its own sake, but also in the dynastic interests of the prince. According to Seneca, mercy should be considered the first amongst the virtues, not only by those who emphasise the natural sociability of man, but also by those who take account only of individual self-interest, 'whose words and deeds all look to their own advantage'.[10] So, whereas tyranny is always unstable, merciful rule is both legitimate and secure.

MACHIAVELLI

Seneca's *De clementia* was the model for the early Renaissance mirror-for-princes literature of which Machiavelli's *The Prince* is the most famous example.[11] And although he refers to *pietà* rather than *clemenza*, Machiavelli implicitly works with the same understandings of mercy and cruelty as Seneca, and accepts that these two poles define the range of possible behaviour for princes toward their subjects. Like Seneca, he takes as a working assumption the idea that cruelty will usually make a prince feared and that mercy will ensure that he is loved. So the question whether it is better to be cruel or merciful can be answered with reference to its consequences: whether it is better to be feared or to be loved.

Although Machiavelli accepts the terms in which Seneca sets up the question, he systematically attempts to overturn his conclusions. Seneca had argued that if the tyrant follows Caligula's motto 'Let them hate, if only they fear', he becomes trapped in a vicious circle: 'since he is hated because he is feared, he wishes to be feared because he is hated'.[12] Machiavelli, however, reaffirms the wisdom of Caligula's dictum, arguing that 'it is far better to be feared than loved if you cannot be both' because bonds of love are easily broken by self-interest, whereas fear is strengthened by the prospect of punishment, and much more reliable. All a prince needs to do to avoid being hated is to have the reputation for mercy rather than cruelty.[13]

Machiavelli seeks to show that it is possible to have a reputation for mercy without actually displaying it—either by tempering cruelty with occasional humanity, or simply by using cruelty against itself. To the merciful example of Julius Caesar in Rome, Machiavelli counterposes Cesare Borgia as an exemplar of successful cruelty in the Romagna. There, he had first used the services of the ruthless Remirro de Orco, and then, aware that Remirro would surely make himself hated, had him cut in two in the piazza in Cesena. The two acts of cruelty cancelled each other out as effectively as clemency would have done, and left the people of the Romagna 'at once appeased and stupefied' by the brutal spectacle. Contrasting Cesare Borgia's restoration of order to the Romagna with the feeble Florentines whose compassion allowed Pistoia to be devastated, Machiavelli argues that such outcomes show that, on balance, it is better to be feared than loved, and that cruelty is to be preferred to mercy, especially for new rulers, for whom it is unavoidable.[14]

Seneca had argued that virtue is also in the interests of the prince, but Machiavelli refutes this. He gives a long list of complementary vices and virtues, 'some cruel some compassionate (*pietoso*)', and argues that, while it is good to have a reputation for the virtues, a prince must of necessity embrace the vices to secure his position.[15] Mercy is not always in the interest of a prince: 'A prince, especially a new prince, cannot observe all those things which give men a reputation for virtue, because in order to maintain his state (*mantenere lo stato*) he is often forced to act in defiance of good faith, of charity, of kindness, of religion'.[16] It follows from this that mercy cannot provide the basis for a king/tyrant distinction, because any such distinction will be inherently unstable. Politics has to be governed by interest, not virtue, and it will therefore sometimes be in the interest of a king to become a tyrant in order to continue to rule.

Aristotle had argued that a tyrant rules in his own interest whereas the king rules for the common good. But Machiavelli, while acknowledging the common good when it comes to republics, never mentions it in *The Prince*. In a monarchy, by definition, the interests of the state are those of its ruler, not those of the people.[17] In response to Aristotle, Machiavelli argues that any prince must rule in their own interest qua ruler, otherwise they will cease to rule: 'If a prince wants to maintain his rule he must be prepared not to be virtuous, and to make use of this or not according to need'. Seneca had claimed that 'a reign that is cruel is stormy and overcast with gloom'. Machiavelli argues that it is not virtue that makes the weather, but *fortuna*: a ruler who can adapt to change will succeed; one who does not is doomed to fail.[18]

If Machiavelli is right, any idea that mercy might be a political virtue, let alone the primary political virtue, will inevitably founder in the uncertain and brutal realities of politics. Like later political realists, Machiavelli wants 'to represent things as they are in a real truth, rather than as they are imagined' and 'to say something that will prove of practical use'. And that means acknowledging that 'the gulf between how one should live and how one does live is so wide that a man who neglects what is actually done for what should be done moves toward self-destruction rather than self-preservation'.[19] For Machiavelli, there is no meaningful political theory that is not also a survival strategy. Hirschman claims that he was the original source of the belief in the primacy of the interests.[20]

MONTAIGNE

The counter-argument starts with Montaigne, but not because he finds any more certainty in an uncertain world than does Machiavelli.[21] On the contrary, he shares much of Machiavelli's scepticism—not just about the pretensions of religion, but of humanity itself. As the *Apology for Raymond Sebond* makes clear, human beings place too much confidence in their reason and exaggerate the differences between men and animals. In contrast, Montaigne sets out to 'make men feel the emptiness, the vanity, the nothingness of

Man'.[22] There is no firm foundation for human knowledge, for the senses themselves are fallible.[23] Even the power of reason has little authority over the body: How much use is philosophy in enabling you to walk the tightrope? And yet it is in our embodied state that reason and virtue are put to the test: 'the power and actions of our souls must be examined not elsewhere but here, at home in our bodies'.[24]

For Montaigne, scepticism leaves us with our physical embodiment, and so it is the body that ultimately determines our priorities. Of these, the avoidance of pain is the first, for 'pain is the worst disaster that can befall our being'.[25] It is this vulnerable physicality that provides the basis for Montaigne's repudiation of Machiavelli. Scepticism points to materialism as well as to pragmatism, and, for Montaigne, Machiavelli's opportunism is always going to run aground in the realities of our embodiment. Utility shouldn't necessarily have the last word; outcomes are always uncertain, save in that they are bodily outcomes, and there are some outcomes against which the body will revolt, whether in the case of self or others.

Montaigne notices such reactions in himself, even in the context of activities that he otherwise approves or even enjoys: 'Among the vices, both by nature and judgement I have a cruel hatred of cruelty, as the ultimate vice of them all'. He relishes the hunt, but 'cannot bear to hear a hare squealing when [his] hounds get their teeth into it'. Because he cannot overcome it, this involuntary sympathetic reaction has an impact on his actions: 'I hardly ever catch a beast alive without restoring it to its fields'.[26] It is this shared physicality of humans and of other creatures that becomes the basis for a principle of conduct: 'My horror of cruelty thrusts me deeper into clemency than any example of clemency ever could draw me'.[27]

How then does Montaigne deal with Machiavelli's argument that such fine feelings are all very well, but, given the uncertainty of fortune, incompatible with rulership? Montaigne had clearly read Machiavelli; he refers to him by name and knows how his arguments go, referring pointedly to 'those writers nowadays who, when drawing up the duties of a prince have considered only what is good for the affairs of state, placing that before his fidelity and conscience'. But he turns Machiavelli against himself, using the argument from uncertainty as a response to Machiavelli's advocacy of advantage over principle. Such counsel might be relevant in the case of a prince who could secure an enduring advantage 'by one single act of deception, one failure to keep his word'. In practice, however, princes are never playing a one-shot game, and they are liable to forfeit their illicit gains in subsequent moves: 'that first profit entails infinite subsequent losses, putting that prince, by his first breach of trust, beyond all negotiations'.[28]

Montaigne is enough of a realist to concede that Machiavelli's advice may sometimes work, but he shifts the ground of the argument. Rather than uncertainty showing that you must act according to interest, uncertainty suggests that you are unlikely to be able to assess long-term interests; acting according to conviction is just as good a bet in terms of outcomes and a much surer one in terms of conscience and status. As a general principle, therefore, 'raison d'état' must be rejected: 'We wrongly adduce the honour and beauty of an activity from its usefulness, and our conclusion is wrong if we reckon that all are bound to perform it, and that it is honourable for each to do so, provided it be useful'.[29]

He applies this argument to mercy, citing examples of clemency to would-be assassins, all with wildly differing outcomes. Montaigne is philosophical about the results: if things turn out badly for someone, that is no reason to condemn his good intentions, as fortune might have turned against him anyway. The assassination of Julius Caesar was not an argument against his practice of winning people over through acts of mercy.[30] As Montaigne's personal hero, the Spartan Epaminondas, had demonstrated, there is no special merit in sacrificing virtue or private obligation in the interests of the state.[31] And Montaigne himself admits to having followed his example: 'I am such a coward about hurting people that I cannot do it even to serve a rational end: when circumstances have required me to pass sentences on criminals I have preferred not to enforce justice'.[32]

Seneca had maintained that mercy was aligned with interest, Machiavelli that it was not. Montaigne partially accepts the latter argument, but claims that in an uncertain world there is no good reason for interest to have the final say. By allowing that mercy might be preferable even though contrary to interest, Montaigne reinvents Seneca's argument in the light of Machiavelli. The case for mercy is now grounded elsewhere. Scepticism undermines false certainties about both ourselves and the future. In these circumstances, it is not rational self-interest that is the only certainty, but the body's will to live and its involuntary abhorrence of pain. The desire to avoid cruelty is not just intellectual but physical. You cannot not want it. Mercy is therefore a biopolitical rather than a social or moral virtue. Rather than being opposed to political realism, mercy is a concession to it—a recognition of the material basis of existence, the adventitious quality of things, and the illusive nature of human order.

SHKLAR

Montaigne's arguments lie dormant until they are picked up by Judith Shklar in two essays, 'Putting Cruelty First' and 'The Liberalism of Fear'.[33] He had been motivated by the wars of religion, but she had the atrocities of the mid-twentieth century to deal with, and, if anything, she gives Montaigne's arguments more weight than he does. According to Shklar, cruelty is 'the wilful inflicting of physical pain on a weaker being in order to cause anguish and fear', and fear 'is as universal as it is physiological ... a mental as well as a physical reaction ... common to animals as well as to human beings'.[34] That is why cruelty has to come first. Wherever cruelty is possible, and it almost always is, finding some way to avoid it will be more important than anything else. But that involves transforming the way we think about politics. Putting cruelty first means that 'the basic units of political life are not discursive and reflecting persons, nor friends and enemies, nor patriotic soldier-citizens, nor energetic litigants, but the weak and the powerful'.[35]

If that is the case, why was cruelty never the focus of political theory before? Why, according to Shklar, was Montaigne the first person to grapple with it? One answer might be that political theory was written by and for the powerful rather than the weak. But Shklar offers another explanation. Putting cruelty first is a response to the modern disenchantment of the world, a world that is, as Montaigne writes, 'incapable of curing itself'.[36] It is devoid of any appeal to the transcendental or even to reasons of state. It emerges from the routine experience of cruelty in both private and public life, and with nothing to justify cruelty, there is no appeal 'to any order other than that of actuality'. It is part of everyday life assessed in terms of everyday life, 'a purely human verdict upon human conduct'. That is why hating cruelty more than anything else requires 'a radical rejection of both religious and political conventions', perhaps even the suspension of reason.[37] It is an extreme position in the sense that putting cruelty first is what is done in extremis.

According to Shklar, the first three of Montaigne's essays all engage Machiavelli, with Montaigne reading *The Prince* not as potential ruler or consigliere, but as a loser in the struggle for power, and asking the questions that potential victims of a victorious prince might ask, such as, 'Is it better to plead for mercy or display defiance?'[38] However, Shklar's emphasis on Montaigne's identification with victims positions her discussion of cruelty somewhat differently. Montaigne is aware of himself not just as a potential victim but also, perhaps more realistically—since he was a hunter and a magistrate—a potential perpetrator of cruelty. For Montaigne, therefore, there is a remedy at hand for cruelty: mercy. And in writing about the topic he makes repeated reference to mercy as well, consciously putting himself in dialogue not just with Machiavelli, but with Seneca too.

Shklar ignores all of this, for she has another remedy. Although she acknowledges that putting cruelty first goes well beyond liberalism, she maintains that liberalism is grounded in the beliefs of early defenders of religious toleration, who saw in cruelty an absolute evil.[39] Cruelty is foundational for liberalism because it inspires fear, and because that fear 'is so universal, moral claims based on its prohibition have an immediate appeal and can gain recognition without much argument'. It is on this basis that 'the prohibition of cruelty can be universalized and recognized as a necessary condition of the dignity of persons'.[40] But this 'liberalism of fear', as Shklar calls it, remains nonutopian; it is focused on the prevention of harm, and the freedom it secures is above all 'freedom from the abuse of power and intimidation of the defenceless'.[41]

The liberalism of fear is closer to Berlin's negative liberty—though it more readily allows that harm is often mediated through economic and environmental factors—than it is to the liberalism of natural rights or the liberalism of personal development.[42] What makes it recognisably a form of liberalism is its individualism (it has no place for a communal self, or sense of the common good), and, in Shklar's version, its reliance on theories of rights and systems of rules to protect the individual against those who are more powerful, especially the state. Since the place where the individual comes face to face with the power of the state is the courtroom, what a liberalism of fear must seek to provide is a legal system protective of individual rights.[43]

However, it is by no means clear that the foundation Shklar has identified will support the political theory she hopes to build on it. It is one thing to put cruelty first, quite another to suggest that putting cruelty first is a sufficient basis for political liberalism in any conventional sense of the term.[44] Nevertheless, putting cruelty first may still be a viable starting point for thinking about politics. It means putting the involuntary responses of the body before the transcendental claims of political theory, and a willingness 'to ask the likeliest victims, the least powerful persons' in order to understand 'what cruelties are to be endured at any place and at any time'.[45] There are many things for which this might seem to be an unsuitable foundation, but politics is not one of them, for, whatever else it is, politics is a collective scheme for keeping (at least some) people alive and functioning when they might otherwise be suffering or dead. The bodies of the vulnerable are always its raw material.

WILLIAMS

Shklar's determination to put cruelty first opened up a space in political theory that has never been completely filled. The philosopher who made the most sustained (though fragmentary) attempt to take Shklar's ideas forward was perhaps Bernard Williams.[46] He argued that what distinguishes the liberalism of fear from other liberalisms is the fact that it deals not in ideals (rights, virtues, etc.) but rather with the real stuff of politics, its materials the 'only certainly universal materials of politics: power, powerlessness, fear, cruelty, a universalism of negative capacities'. Like

Machiavelli's *Prince* it 'does not displace politics, but is understood only in the presence of politics, and as addressing its listeners in the presence of their politics'.[47]

In this respect, the liberalism of fear differs from political theories (e.g., utilitarianism and Rawlsian liberalism) that are more like 'applied morality'. Williams calls this approach 'political moralism', and he rejects it.[48] According to him, political morality compounds the mistakes made in conflating ethics with morality in the first place. Ethical thought has generally sought to replace thick (i.e., local, descriptive) concepts with thin (i.e., universal, abstract) ones, and then use them to provide a personal morality composed of obligatory voluntary acts.[49] This morality has then been extended to politics, because the power of the state has fostered the illusion 'that the territory of legal control, and the sphere of a significant ethical life, should be the same', and that some set of abstract and universally applicable rules should govern both.[50]

Against this Williams argues that rationality does not require us to exchange thick for thin ethical concepts, and that thin concepts are in any case incapable of supplying public justification for either private or political morality. The attempt to find an Archimedean point from which all moral dilemmas can be resolved objectively is fundamentally misconceived. There is no single set of ideas that 'will represent the demands of ethics in all the spheres to which ethical experience applies'.[51] So what does that leave us with as far as politics is concerned? A form of political realism, which takes the values and virtues of politics to be immanent within the practice of politics itself, rather than a set of moral principles that can be applied to politics. And since the actual practice of politics is subject to considerable local and historical variation, this means that those values and virtues are very liable to differ according to the historical and political contexts from which they emerge.

The various practices of politics pose their own questions, but there is one question that all politics has to answer. According to Williams, this 'first political question' is the Hobbesian one regarding 'the securing of order, protection, safety, trust, and the conditions of cooperation'. The question is not 'first in the sense that once solved it never has to be solved again', but in the sense that a solution 'is required all the time'. It takes priority both because solving it is the condition of posing any other political questions, and because its resolution is necessary for the legitimacy of the state.[52]

Even Hobbes did not think a legitimate state could be a reign of terror, so the first political question creates what Williams calls the Basic Legitimation Demand (BLD), the requirement that the state have a solution to the first political question that is 'acceptable'.[53] The state must offer a justification of its power to each subject, such that there is no one individual or group so radically disadvantaged with reference to 'what someone can fear' that they have reason to revolt.

Although justifications may differ according to local circumstances, they have this in common: 'The power of coercion offered simply as the power of coercion cannot justify its own use'. Therefore, 'one sufficient condition of their being a (genuine) demand for justification is this: A coerces B and claims that B would be wrong to fight back.... By doing this, A claims that his actions transcend the conditions of warfare, and this gives rise to a demand for justification of what A does'.[54]

The BLD obviously arises only in situations in which the dominated could conceivably offer some resistance, however futile or suicidal. But Williams argues that justification must go beyond mere power and make sense to us as 'a structure of authority which we think we should accept'.[55] We acknowledge as legitimate what makes sense to us here and now as a legitimation of power as authority, and the legitimation offered suffices if it makes sense in some time and place on any ground other than terror. This excludes acceptance produced through terror itself, even if mediated through ideology. Were there, for example, contented slaves who seemingly did not share the desires that other people had at that time, we would be entitled to ask whether and how that contentment was justified, for 'acceptance of a justification does not count if the acceptance itself is produced by the coercive power which is supposedly being justified'.[56]

The BLD is, then, 'not a morality prior to politics … it is a claim that is inherent in there being such a thing as politics'. A situation in which 'one lot of people [is] terrorizing another lot of people is not … a political situation: it is, rather, the situation which the … political is in the first place supposed to alleviate (replace)'.[57] Williams therefore posits a distinction between situations where there is domination with justification and those where there is none. In the former case, there is acceptance and no reason to revolt, while in the latter there is effectively a state of war. On this view, all human association involves either politics or war, and 'it can be an illuminating question … to ask how far and in what respects, a given society of the past is an example of the human capacity for intelligible order, or of the human tendency to unmediated coercion'.[58]

SLAVES, HELOTS, AND CHILDREN

Williams's identification of politics with peace as opposed to war is persuasive, and it is adopted in the argument that follows. But his clear theoretical distinction between legitimate domination and war proves difficult to maintain. It is hard to argue that the BLD has to be satisfied for there to be peace rather than war when forms of domination for which little or no justification is offered can, as political and legal forms, remain largely uncontested for centuries or even millennia (e.g., the various forms of slavery, empire, and patriarchy). Williams acknowledges that there is a distinction to be made between 'reasons for stopping warfare' and 'reasons given by a claim for authority'.[59] But if they are not the same then there must be situations in which warfare has stopped, no claim for authority is made, yet domination continues. So what is the difference between legitimate dominion and domination that you have no pressing reason to rebel against (i.e., is at least temporarily accepted) but offers no particular justification?

Consider a form of domination like slavery, in which the power of coercion is taken to be self-justifying (as a prisoner of war you become a slave). This obviously does not meet the criteria of the BLD, because 'the power of coercion cannot justify its own use'. It therefore provides a useful example of pure domination against which to test Williams's hypothesis. According to Williams, unmediated coercion cannot produce a political order, and is rather 'a form of internalized warfare'.[60] However, numerous historical examples suggest that slavery has been able to provide the framework for stable political structures in which it is not just the coercive base, but so fully integrated that slaves themselves could function as *political* actors (e.g., as grand vizier in the Ottoman empire). However unacceptable it may be in moral terms, slavery (or empire, or patriarchy) has sometimes been sufficiently accepted for the societies in which it is found to be at peace.

Satisfying the BLD just does not seem to be necessary for what is recognisably politics, and it does not appear to be sufficient either. Let us suppose that some justification is supplied that momentarily passes what Williams calls the 'Critical Theory Test', in that it 'makes sense' at the time, and is delivered by instructors whose authority is plausible independent of the justificatory theory that they teach —say, the Aristotelian theory of slavery or scientific racism in the nineteenth century (to cite the two serious attempts to justify a practice that otherwise functioned without one).[61] Both are intrinsically worthless, but in their time their plausibility did not depend wholly on the institution they purported to explain. In such cases it seems impossible to argue that 'unmediated coercion' became 'intelligible order' just because someone came up with a temporarily plausible explanation, or to explain what happened when that plausibility eroded.

Formerly acceptable justifications are often disregarded without power being contested (many traditional forms of authority survive loss of faith in their foundation myths). On the other hand, it is often the case that provinces secede, civil wars break out, or rebellions occur without any obvious challenge to the existing justifications of authority. In such cases, it is not necessarily that legitimation has broken down. In medieval and early modern Europe, rebellions against monarchs were rarely the work of republicans. True believers can easily find themselves at war with religious authorities they accept; even ancient slave revolts were not against the institution per se. Despite the presence of many highly educated slaves in antiquity, the sources of rebellion were more often to be found in the body than the soul. As Bulla Felix is reported to have said: 'Tell your masters that they should feed their slaves enough so that they do not turn to a life of banditry'.[62] Revenge on the poorly legitimated is not so common as revenge on the cruel.

According to Williams, unless those with power have 'something to say' that plausibly justifies that power, they will be treating those over whom they exercise power merely as enemies, 'as the ancient Spartiates, consistently, treated the helots whom they had subjugated'.[63] But in practice the friend-enemy distinction is a very fluid one, and having 'something to say' does not seem to explain the resulting pattern. Thus, Williams elides significant differences between the condition of the helots during the Spartans' annual cull; their situation during the rest of the year (when they were not protected but were unlikely to be arbitrarily killed); and the position of slaves, who although individually the property of their masters were part of the framework of the law.

The example can be taken further. The position of Roman slaves was in some respects similar to that of children, in that both lacked legal rights and could be put to death by their masters or fathers. Williams presumably would not want to argue that the relationship of Roman parents and their children was one of warfare, but it is clear that the predicament of the child differs from that of the household slave only in degree. Within the continuum from hunted helot to Roman child, one thing remains the same: they can be killed with impunity, yet, according to Williams, at one extreme it is war, at the other peace. But not only is there no absolute distinction between war and peace to be found here; it is impossible to argue that it is the justification offered that intervenes to makes the difference. Having 'something to say' does not seem to come in to it.[64]

MERCY AGAIN

If the basis of politics is 'what someone can fear', it is the function of politics to deal with that fear in such a way that coercive force can be accepted rather than rejected as a reign of terror. Williams claims that this happens as the result of a justification that makes enough sense to the subjugated for them to acknowledge the legitimacy of power. But on examination this explanation does not seem to work, and 'making sense' is revealed to be neither a necessary nor a sufficient condition of politics. Is there another way of answering the first political question? Williams's approach to political theory is inspired by Shklar's liberalism of fear, which, in turn, is grounded in the fear and abhorrence of cruelty identified by Montaigne. Making the question of order the first political question is Williams's way of putting cruelty first. But for Montaigne, mercy was the only possible way to eliminate cruelty, and with it the cruel fear of further cruelty. Might mercy rather than justification be what is required?

The answer will depend on whether we think that the transition from war to politics primarily involves reconciling people to fear or giving them less to be afraid of. Does accepting domination mean having some reason, 'which we think we should accept', to go along with it other than (i.e., in addition to) sheer terror? Or does it simply involve having less to fear from domination itself and so experiencing something less than (i.e., instead of) sheer terror? To answer the question we might consider these two possibilities:

1. A coerces B and claims that B would be wrong to fight back (legitimacy) and B does not fight back.
2. A coerces B and claims that B would be ill-advised to fight back (threat) and B does not fight back.

Williams argues that the first is politics and the second is war. At first glance it might appear that B is being offered two distinct reasons for not fighting back.

However, the two are less distinct than might appear, for coercion (which is present in both) is itself nothing other than a threat that you would be ill-advised not to heed. So both are threats, though the first purports to be a justified threat.

Effective threats necessarily involve a differential between harm done and harm that might be done. Combine either (1) or (2) with 'A does all the harm to B that they can' and the threat no longer works, because there is by definition nothing else that A could do to harm B, so the threat is empty. It is therefore assumed in both cases that 'A coerces B while doing less harm than they might' and that there is some additional harm that could be done. The potential maximum level of harm is always the same (the powerful may kill you) but the actual level of harm is very variable. This raises the question of whether the difference between threats effective on the basis of fear alone and threats accepted for some other reason reflects the actual level of harm involved. After all, the difference between a helot and a Roman child lies not in the worst that might happen to them, but in the way that they are routinely treated—not in the fear of what might happen but in the everyday experience of fear. Might actual harm be a factor in the acceptance of domination, quite independent of any justification that is offered?

Harm does not refer to a reduction in aggregate well-being but a degree of injury to individuals and their life chances that they would naturally seek to prevent. Obviously a situation in which 'A coerces B while doing all the harm that they can' is going to be no more acceptable than it is effective. In most cases, however, the harm that is in the interest of the powerful is less than the maximum possible. Indeed, the normal level of harm may be no more than the level of violence sufficient to deter revolt. But given that harm is something that people want to avoid, no level of harm can in itself be permanently acceptable. In these circumstances, coercion requires that a threat be constantly renewed, and that renewal necessarily takes one of two forms: it is either a threat to increase harm beyond its normal level, or a reduction of harm combined with the threat to resume harm at or above the normal level (the coronation pardon or amnesty is an example of the latter). Both may be effective. But only one of the two is liable to be accepted on the basis of something other than fear. In the former case, the potential for fear is augmented and the level of harm remains the same; in the latter, the potential for fear is still there, but the level of actual harm is reduced. Someone might plausibly find the latter situation acceptable not just because they were afraid of something worse, but because their situation was better than it was before.

This suggests that to be accepted on some basis other than fear alone, a threat has to be made from a position in which the actual harm being done to the relatively powerless (rather than the potential harm being threatened) is less than it normally would be, perhaps less than it would be in the sole interests of the powerful to do. Of course, this makes acceptance heavily dependent on context. But to give the powerless a motivation to accept their relative powerlessness, at least something has been conceded by the powerful that would not normally be conceded. Without this, it is impossible to see what motive other than fear the powerless could actually have for accepting it. And if, as Machiavelli supposes, the norm and the interests of the powerful will otherwise tend to converge, that means at least one thing has to be different to the way it would be if the powerful ruled solely in their own interests.

Mercy, too, depends on the differential between potential and actual harm, and involves someone doing less harm than they might, or less than would normally be done, so all threats accepted on a basis other than fear are to some degree merciful (though it does not follow from this that all merciful threats are acceptable, or that all mercy is always against the interests of power). But if acceptability necessarily involves mercy, then there may be no absolute difference between the things that make a threat effective and those that make it acceptable. In which case, might power be accepted by those over whom it is exercised on the basis of mercy alone?

This is the implication of Seneca's argument, as becomes clear from the parallel he draws between slave-ownership and sovereignty in *De clementia*.[65] But whereas Aristotle offers a justification for slavery, Seneca does not. In one of the letters addressed to Lucilius, he goes out of his way to undermine any ontological basis for the distinction between master and slave: ' "They are slaves," people declare. Nay, rather they are men.... your slave sprang from the same stock, is smiled upon by the same skies, and on equal terms with yourself breathes, lives, and dies. It is just as possible for you to see in him a free-born man as for him to see in you a slave'.[66] But although Seneca offers no justification for slavery at all, he does not repudiate it either. It is an institution that exists within his society and it can be maintained by following this advice: 'Treat your inferiors as you would be treated by your betters', for only in that way will you not make enemies of them.[67]

Of course, this does not constitute a legitimation for slavery as an institution. But that is not what Seneca is seeking. His concern is rather more basic—how to ensure that you are not murdered by your own slaves—and his answer is instructive. Mercy was the standard justification for slavery in that slaves were, in theory at least, those whose lives had been spared in war. Were a single act of mercy sufficient to ensure the master's safety, then the fact that the master had not killed the slave in the first place would suffice. And if continuity alone were required, then that would be fulfilled by the master's decision not to kill the slave from one moment to the next. However, mercy needs to be demonstrated continuously, and in new ways, as the situation demands. Treating the slave as you might treat a friend means maintaining a disposition that is always open to the possibility of exceeding any previous norm of kindness and generosity. The same holds true for the prince in relation to his citizens, for, just as cruelty is avenged by slaves, despite the risk of crucifixion, so too 'nations ... extirpate the cruelty of tyrants'.[68] Roman authors referred to the continuing disposition to mercy as goodness, *bonitas*, and Seneca himself attributes it to Nero, arguing that it is through his goodness that he will demonstrate 'not that the state is his, but that he is the state's'.[69]

Yet how persuasive can mercy be? Can it ever really be enough? We take for granted that it is sufficient for domestic animals and children. That does not mean that dogs never bite the hand that feeds them, just that merciful treatment is in and of itself the most reliable way to ensure compliance and trust (without any form of justification being necessary). Why should it not work for adult human beings as well? Like Williams, Seneca is trying to answer the first question of politics: How can you ensure domination without rebellion? But to claim that it is mercy that permits 'the securing of order, protection, safety, trust, and the conditions of cooperation' is to offer a very different response to the one Williams envisages in the BLD. On this view, the acceptability of power derives not from any agreement or explanation or argument or myth, but from the simple fact that it is not exercised to the full. Putting up with subordination and accepting a justification are not the same, and the former is all that is required for peace rather than war. What needs to be accepted is not the justification but the power itself. There is nothing moral about this: no 'ought' is involved, and perhaps no thought either. Mercy is to be found within coercion, in the forbearance of the powerful in the exercise of power.

Williams is looking for a clear distinction between peace and war, friends and enemies. But Seneca's account of mercy will not yield one. The question of whether power is legitimate will have a different type of answer to the question of whether power is acceptable. The former is an either-or question—someone either is or is not the legitimate ruler, and the answer to the question is subject neither to vagueness nor to change across time; the latter is always a matter of degree. Whereas giving consent or accepting a justification is a threshold concept yielding a yes-no response, mercy and the acceptance it wins is always partial and graduated, and the degree of acceptance accorded to it proportionate to the degree of mercy shown.

It is in this sense that mercy is sufficient for peace. As Cicero's claim that Julius Caesar conquered 'the conditions and the violent privileges of victory itself' implies, for any form of power over there is potentially a degree of mercy in the exercise of that power that would make it more acceptable to those over whom it is exercised. This may seem an unwarranted claim with unwelcome consequences, but if power could be exercised as though it did not exist, then there could be no reason why it would not also be acceptable. Thus it might be claimed not only that some degree of mercy is always necessary for domination to be accepted (in the sense that no one wants to risk their lives to challenge it), but also that for every form of domination there is some additional degree of mercy that will be sufficient for it to become more acceptable.

Is this any more plausible than Williams's suggestion that what is required is legitimation? Let's suppose there are two neighbouring plantations. In one the master treats the slaves with unrelenting cruelty, but all share a belief system that justifies his domination. In the other, with no justification for his domination save that he has the means to maintain it, the master treats the slaves with kindness and consideration. In both cases the slaves appear restive, so the masters offer each other some advice. As a result, the cruel master starts to act with consideration, and the mild one offers what passes for a good reason for slavery. Which of these two changes would provide some motivation for greater acceptance of their lot by the slaves themselves? In the first place the slaves are given the option of being treated like friends rather than tools;

in the second they are offered a belief system that justifies not the mildness with which they are treated but rather their subjugation itself. As this example makes clear, mercy makes a material difference even if there is an existing justification, whereas providing a justification for slavery where none was previously offered adds to, rather than subtracts from, its burden.

ADDRESS

Not only is Williams's answer to the first political question unconvincing, it is not clear to what extent any idea of 'legitimacy' or 'justification' is compatible with his political realism. Suppose that there is a rule of cruel and unmediated coercion. The people get together and sign a petition to their rulers; it reads 'Give us a reason for our suffering'. If anything, that is an ethical (perhaps a theological) rather than a political request, and any response to it that provides a plausible legitimation must have rather different premises to those of political realism or the liberalism of fear. Williams argues in the name of political realism for the primacy of the BLD over any political moralism. But perhaps he was not enough of a realist to accept the consequences of his own thinking here, for mercy rather than legitimacy seems to offer a more appropriate response to the first political question, in that it deals in the 'universal materials of politics: power, powerlessness, fear, cruelty' rather than abstract justifications.

This becomes clearer if we try to make Williams's argument work on its own terms. In practice, he suggests, here and now in modernity, what constitutes legitimacy (i.e., what makes sense to most people) is liberalism: Legitimacy + Modernity = Liberalism.[70] He does not say so explicitly, but he presumably means the 'liberalism of fear' (LOF), because whereas other liberalisms require the support of political morality, a liberalism of fear could (given that it is focused on the avoidance of terror) be developed solely to satisfy the BLD and be said to satisfy it completely. But if the LOF is the way the BLD is formulated in modernity, how would that work?

Given that the BLD requires a justification for domination, one way to throw the question into relief is to consider it in relation to Williams's earlier claim that we should ask of any pretended justification to whom, against what, and from where it is addressed.[71] In the case of a justification of the ethical life, the assumed answer to the question 'Against what?' might be 'The amoralist', somebody who is sceptical about the grounds, purpose, and benefits of the ethical. But the answer to 'To whom?' is other members of the ethical community, for the 'aim of the discourse is not to deal with someone who will not listen to it [i.e., the amoralist], but to reassure, strengthen and give insight to those who will'.[72] According to Williams, justifications of the ethical life cannot be addressed to the amoralist from an Archimedean perspective to compel them to reconsider their position or actions; they rather address other members of their own ethical community from the perspective of rational action.

In the BLD, the justification of its power that the state has to offer to each of its subjects functions rather differently.[73] How would the same questions be answered? The 'To whom' question is easy: the state is addressing each subject. 'Against what?' The impulse to fight back. 'From where?' A position of power. In the BLD, every subject is addressed not as a fellow member of an ethical community (to reinforce solidarity against outsiders) but rather as potential enemies themselves. Here perhaps is a key difference between ethics and politics. Political justifications are justifications that make the difference between peace and war; they are addressed from determinate political or strategic positions, and they are addressed to, and must be made persuasive to, those they are against—potential enemies. Unlike the amoralist (who is more likely to be a mild-mannered sceptic than a psychopath), the potential enemy cannot be ignored.

If the BLD is compatible with the LOF, then that compatibility should manifest itself in terms of address. And if the LOF is something other than a political morality, then it too should make a political address. Indeed, Williams describes it as 'addressing its listeners in the presence of their politics'.[74] But it is not clear that this will work in the way that he suggests.

He distinguishes the LOF from political moralities addressed to the empowered agents who might be expected to put their ideals into practice, and argues that the LOF speaks more widely to humanity instead. But this turns the LOF into ethics rather than politics, for, whereas the amoralist can be ignored, the tyrant and the potential rebel cannot. In politics, unlike ethics, you have to address what you are against from where you are. As Shklar emphasises, putting cruelty first means asking 'the likeliest victims, the least powerful persons'. So if it is to be symmetrical with the BLD, the LOF should be a protest against cruelty addressed from the position of potential victims to the powerful who are likely to harm them.

There is, in other words, a contradiction between the asymmetrical situation presupposed by the first political question, and Williams's proposed solution to it—a justification that makes sense to everyone in the political community. Unlike an ethical justification offered to other members of a community, the solution to the first political question requires the powerful and their subjects to address each other from different positions. So if, as Williams implies, the first political question is satisfied by the LOF, it can only be satisfied in a way that is congruent with mercy, for mercy, too, is always sought from the powerful by the weak. As the example of Sánchez Mazas reveals, there is no need for a word to be spoken on either side. But if there is, and the least powerful address the most powerful, then this may involve some reorientation in what we think political theory involves.

In the ancient world, the form of address that led to mercy was supplication, a sometimes ritualised appeal by, or on behalf of, the mistreated, the defeated, or the dead. Self-abasement is not necessary, but any political address that performs this function will have a distinctive tone and orientation.[75] Seneca's essay addressed to Nero might itself count as an example, a preemptive act of supplication written on behalf of the Roman people and, as it turned out, the philosopher himself. Supplication is a form of persuasion that does not rely on power, or the immediate threat of violence, but only on the potential for mutual comprehension between those who have power and those who do not. In Monteverdi's opera, it is the music in which Orpheus addresses the gods of the underworld.[76]

MACHIAVELLI AGAIN

Williams's political realism takes us back to mercy because if the liberalism of fear is to satisfy the first political question, mercy is required. However, this should not come as too much of a surprise, for it was the ancient debate about mercy and cruelty that gave rise to political realism in the first place.[77] The question Williams sets himself—what makes the difference between war and politics within the state—is the modern equivalent of the ancient one of what constitutes the difference between a tyrant and king. The difference between a king and a tyrant is not their claim to royal legitimacy (that is the difference between a king and a usurper), but rather their actions. And if it is mercy that makes the difference, then any answer to the first political question cannot but be a restatement of Seneca's original argument.[78]

But there is a difference in context. Seneca argued that the difference between a king and a tyrant was itself a matter of honour, but that the consequence of merciful rule was also a greater degree of security, with less to fear from those whom one has wronged. In the first political question Williams elides the two. The difference between successful domination and politics is not a moral or aesthetic one that happens to have beneficial consequences; rather, the difference between the two lies in those consequences, in that if domination is contested it is just that, whereas if it is accepted, then it is politics.

The argument develops this way because of Machiavelli's intervention. Machiavelli had rejected Seneca's account on the grounds that whatever might be said for honour, or any other virtue, successful domination was a more secure basis for princely rule than mercy could ever be. In politics, all that matters is power itself and the best way to maintain it, so the successful conduct of politics over time demands a realism untempered by moral or aristocratic codes of behaviour.

In response, Montaigne argues that revulsion to cruelty is a universal, almost physical response, and that cruelty leads to vengeance as often as mercy leads to betrayal. Even if Machiavelli is right to suggest that mercy will give way before political expediency, Montaigne insists that you are always going to need it, and that mercy is an ineradicable part of the reality of politics.

Williams picks up Montaigne's point about cruelty from Shklar, but applies it within a Machiavellian framework: he claims that the liberalism of fear is the very opposite of Machiavelli, and yet that it too is purely about politics rather than morality, because the acceptance of coercion is necessary for peace rather than war.[79] Machiavelli might have sacrificed the tyrant/ king distinction, but despite his insistence on the primacy of war, he continues to acknowledge that there is a difference between war and peace (for peace is necessary to prepare for war).[80] But if mercy is necessary for peace, then only avoiding cruelty insofar as it is in your interest to do so (which is what Machiavelli suggests) can never be enough. In the long run, peace requires more than that—abstaining from cruelty even when it might be in the interest of the prince.

On this account, politics, as opposed to war, is distinguished by restraint in the use of violence even in cases where there are no external moral or cultural restraints. Politics cannot be purely a matter of self-interest without degenerating into constant war.

Machiavelli was wrong to think that politics without morality could mean always acting according to interest alone. Political realism, insofar as it is *political*, comes with built-in constraints. What this amounts to is a different account of the way mercy functions within politics: not as part of a moral code awkwardly accommodated, but rather as the condition of doing politics at all. If it is a virtue, mercy is a political virtue.

2

Mercy may be a political virtue, but how central is it to political theory? It is often claimed that the circumstances of mercy are to be found at the margins of human social experience, and are therefore irrelevant to politics itself. In contrast, the emergence of justice from the circumstances of justice is held to be both necessary and sufficient to account for society. Could the same claim ever be made for mercy? Could mercy account for social order?

Because mercy is always relative and involves doing less harm than you might, or less than you would normally do, it is easy to think that it is a secondary virtue. Insofar as mercy tempers absolute power or established norms of justice, it is natural to assume that it is these that create social order while mercy serves (if it serves any purpose at all) only to soften their impact. Even the argument of the previous chapter presupposes that a potential solution to the problem of order has already been found, and that what is needed is an acceptable solution (otherwise it will turn out to be no solution at all). But, although mercy may be particularly appropriate for the sovereign, because it is to the sovereign that the monopoly of violence is attributed, the circumstances of mercy are not created by sovereignty. The power of coercion is not always centralised. Suppose there is no sovereign; what happens then?[1]

CIRCUMSTANCES OF MERCY

It is worth spelling out in more detail what the circumstances of mercy actually are. Mercy involves doing less harm than you might. So in order to show mercy someone has to have power, and someone else must be vulnerable to that power. But what kind of power are we talking about? It is 'power over' rather than 'power to' because mercy always affects someone else's interests.[2] Power over is a function of the differential between one agent's structural position and capacities and another's, and it arises in cases where one agent has more control over an individual than they do themselves. Even if this power does not necessarily involve having the power to affect someone else's interests negatively (it might involve having the power to impose a choice between indifferent alternatives), it does in the case of mercy, which always supposes the power to harm. In classic cases, mercy is exercised by someone who has the power of life and death over another individual, or the power to do them (or impose upon them) some bodily harm. This is distinct from the power to shape someone else's life in other ways, which is an altogether more complex matter and usually more diffused.

Indeed, it is often difficult to specify all those people who have power over someone's future. The judge who decides whether to impose the death penalty clearly has power over, as does the state governor who alone can commute the sentence; but the prison guard who (like his co-workers) could enable the prisoner to escape is in a more ambiguous position, as is the citizen who might petition the governor for clemency. You can only be said to have power over to the extent that you are able to exercise it. And in many cases power cannot be exercised independently, so it is not just individuals who have power over, but also governments, boards of corporations, juries, local committees, electorates, consumers, collectives, etc. Anybody who can make decisions that could potentially change other lives decisively for the worse has power over others, and this includes the power mediated through the market. One consequence of this is that 'power with' (in which participation and cooperation are part of the construction of agency) may be a form of 'power over', not just directly with regard to the objects of collective action or consumer choice, but other members of the collectivity itself who may be disempowered by the participation or nonparticipation of their fellows.

But what about power over social, economic, ecological, technological, or ideological forces, or combinations of the above, that create the environment in which individuals live?[3] All have the power to impact individual lives negatively, but it makes sense to speak of that power as being exercised more or less mercifully by virtue of its marginal effect on individuals rather than its aggregate outcome. A taxation system that rounds down rather than up to the nearest whole number is more merciful than one that works in the other direction on account of the harm it might do to some vulnerable taxpayers, even though in most cases it won't make much difference either way. A wind farm sited away from a migration route will be more merciful to those birds that might have flown into it if it were not; a belief system that encourages moderation is liable to be more merciful than one that does not by virtue of its effect on the vulnerable.

Mercy can only be shown to the vulnerable because if you are invulnerable you cannot be harmed. And vulnerability, as Martha Fineman has argued, arises primarily from embodiment. It is because we are alive and have bodies that we are all capable of being killed, injured, pained, or prevented from living the life of which we might otherwise be capable. This means that it is important to distinguish cases that affect living beings from those that do not. A program that rounds down fractions may be merciful at the tax office where it affects people, but if the fractions in question are created by some other form of data (e.g., inventory levels) the question would not necessarily arise. Mercy inflects a power that is exercised over life itself.

Unlike autonomy and independence, which are enjoyed only by healthy adults, vulnerability is a universal condition.[4] Even at our least vulnerable, we are still liable to unexpected reversals in health or fortune, still dependent on others for at least some of our physical and emotional needs. However, the universality of vulnerability may disguise the degree to which vulnerabilities range in type and magnitude, and the degree to which one person is vulnerable to another. As Robert Goodin has argued, 'Vulnerability is inherently object and agent specific'. References to vulnerability always involve a 'to what' and a 'to whom'. In which case, to posit the vulnerable subject as a universal figure is in some ways misleading. Vulnerabilities are often a function of someone else's power, and imply that there is some agent capable of choosing 'whether to cause or to avert the threatened harm'.[5]

So although being vulnerable means being at the mercy of someone or something that might cause harm, it is only where there is also power and agency that the vulnerable can receive mercy (as opposed to avoid harm). Of course, the total picture of power/vulnerability is a complex one. Not only is power often exercised through collective action, but we also sometimes become vulnerable as part of a collectivity. However, there is an asymmetry here: exercising power as part of a collectivity is rather different from exercising it as an individual, but, while we may be vulnerable as part of a group or category of persons, that vulnerability is always an individual vulnerability. This points to another asymmetry. Although most people both have power over and are vulnerable to other people, such relationships are very rarely reciprocal, let alone symmetrical. Power is far less evenly distributed than vulnerability, and some people have no (or very little) power over others, while a few individuals have power over many. In contrast, although all are vulnerable, some are vulnerable to everyone, and others vulnerable only to a few.

The circumstances of mercy comprise not just a power relationship, but the potential for certain kinds of action in the context of that relationship. Mercy involves doing less harm than you might or than you would usually do. Harm has to be net (otherwise there could be no appendectomies) and at a threshold that someone would not willingly tolerate indefinitely. Many things and situations are susceptible to change, for better or worse, but not to harm. Most harms will ultimately take a physical toll on a vulnerable individual, though in many cases the route is indirect, and mediated through economic deprivation. One useful way of thinking about harm is therefore the capabilities approach, which is formulated in terms of potentialities.[6] Capability is defined by the ability someone has to do things he or she has reason to value. Harm is a reduction in that capability—i.e., becoming less capable than you were before. To be at the mercy of someone is to find yourself in a position in which your capabilities may be severely limited by the unilateral actions or decisions of another agent.

If that is the case, then being at the mercy of is itself a limitation of capabilities, in that if someone else has the power to reduce your functionings at will, then your ability to plan and achieve your objectives will be circumscribed and your autonomy diminished. Being vulnerable, or at least more vulnerable than you could be, is itself therefore usually a form of harm. There are exceptions, as when the paramedics strap you to the stretcher so that you can be winched to safety, and there is scope for debate about how far they extend. But an important corollary of this is that the circumstances of mercy are often themselves a circumstance of mercy, and although the exercise of mercy may help to eliminate the circumstances of mercy, in most cases increasing power over is intrinsically harmful, so an increase in power over/vulnerability to is by definition a greater harm than normal and in and of itself unmerciful.

However, failure to enhance someone's capabilities does not qualify as harm. Even if you are in a position to do so, failure to bestow a benefit does not leave the other person worse off than they were beforehand. Power to benefit others does not constitute power over, and you cannot act mercifully towards someone you do not have power over. But that distinction becomes blurred in the case of allowing avoidable harm. Having the power to save someone from harm counts as having power over to the degree that you are indeed able to save them. So what about situations (like the classic trolley problems) where you can either allow harm or prevent it by committing a lesser harm? Is this a circumstance of mercy? It would seem like it, because you have power both to commit harm and to allow a harm that only you could prevent, and two distinct sets of people are vulnerable to you. However, they would be better described as two simultaneous but different circumstances of mercy. All that is required for the circumstances of mercy to obtain is that there be a range of possible outcomes and that those outcomes can be ranked according to harm. Comparison but not aggregation is required. So, in situations where acting mercifully to x may entail being unmerciful to y, there is not necessarily any way of aggregating mercy or any need to do so. One consequence of this account is that not everyone has equal potential to act mercifully. Another is that, although those with power over are always in a position to be merciful, it may not be possible to act mercifully towards everyone at the same time.

HUME

Those with the most potential to be merciful are those with the most power over. The most merciful are those who have the most power and do the least harm; the least merciful are those whose power to harm is exercised in full at all times. This is why mercy has long been associated with sovereignty, and is often assumed to be the prerogative of the sovereign alone. However, if mercy is just a ratio between the potential power to harm and the harm done, the circumstances of mercy extend beyond those of sovereignty. Comparable situations arise wherever the inequality of powers is so great that it cannot easily be contested.

Indeed, as Hume's description of the intermingling of two unequal species suggests, such situations can amount to a form of de facto sovereignty:

> Were there a species of creatures intermingled with men, which, though rational, were possessed of such inferior strength, both of body and mind, that they were incapable of all resistance, and could never, upon the highest provocation, make us feel the effects of their resentment; the necessary consequence, I think, is that we should be bound by the laws of humanity to give gentle usage to these creatures, but should not, properly speaking, lie under any restraint of justice with regard to them, nor could they possess any right or property, exclusive of such arbitrary lords.[7]

The situation described here fits the definition of the circumstances of mercy given above. By the 'laws of humanity' Hume refers not to any 'laws', but to the exercise of a virtue that in such circumstances amounts to mercy. Consistently equated with benevolence in the *Enquiry*, 'humanity' is an inclusive term that is aligned with 'gentleness and moderation' against brutality and cruelty, and identified as a virtue only partly conformable to justice.[8] But, although Hume makes humanity the foundation of moral judgement, he maintains that there is no stable, unambiguous example of a sustained social relationship that operates on this basis. He considers the possibility with regard to the relations betweens humans and animals, Europeans and Indians, and men and women.[9] But he quickly disregards them all: animals may not meet the rationality requirement; Europeans dispensed with both humanity and justice in their dealings with colonised peoples; women are adept at undermining male monopolies of power. So none furnishes a clear example of the laws of humanity being followed rather than those of justice.

But Hume is surely too hasty here. There is no need to appeal to the apparently not so remote eventuality that AI robots will come to dominate the human race to find examples of situations in which individuals or categories of persons are effectively defenceless in their dealings with others. Everyone finds themselves in this situation at one time or another, and dependency is just a sort of long-term vulnerability experienced by children, the sick, the old, the disabled, the conquered, and many others whose vulnerability is contingent on their economic circumstances and/or systematic discrimination. Far from being a marginal set of circumstances—rarely or only ambiguously instantiated—these are for many the normal circumstances of everyday life.

However, as Hume emphasises, they are the circumstances not of justice but of mercy: 'Our compassion and kindness the only check, by which they curb our lawless will ... the restraints of justice and property, being totally *useless*, would never have place in so unequal a confederacy'.[10] This is significant because it was to leave the field clear for justice that mercy was excluded (by Hume and others) from legal and political discourse in the eighteenth century. But if, as Hume claims, the circumstances of mercy are incompatible with the principles of justice, then justice cannot operate wherever they hold. A great deal therefore hinges on the question of the relative scope of the circumstances of justice and of mercy.

CIRCUMSTANCES OF JUSTICE

What are the circumstances of justice? According to Hume in the *Treatise*, there are three types of good: the internal satisfaction of our minds, the external advantages of the body, and the enjoyment of possessions. Justice relates to the last of these, as possessions are susceptible to transfer from one person to another in a way that other goods are not. Society is the source of the multiplication of possessions, but as there is an insufficient quantity for everyone's 'desires and necessities', the instability of possession is 'the chief impediment' of society. Justice is therefore designed to remedy the inconveniences consequent upon limited generosity and the scarcity of resources: 'It is only from the selfishness and confined generosity of men, along with the scanty provision [of] nature ... that justice derives its origin'.[11]

However, as he acknowledges in the *Enquiry*, the existence of radically diverse capabilities is only one of the situations in which justice would not apply. In a state of abundance, justice would be irrelevant, because everyone could help themselves to whatever they wanted (as is already the case with air, for example). Conversely, in circumstances of dire need, where there is not enough for everyone, justice is suspended, and it is a case of everyone for themselves. The degree of benevolence also makes a difference: total beneficence would likewise render justice superfluous, for everything could amicably be shared or held in common. On the other hand, should beneficence be completely lacking, so too would be the requirement of justice.[12]

Hume's account of the circumstances of justice might seem to exclude rather a lot, but this has not prevented it from having a decisive role in determining the scope and direction of Anglo-American political theory since the 1970s. Rawls describes Hume's account of the circumstances of justice as 'especially perspicuous' and bases his own upon it. According to

Rawls, the circumstances of justice are just the 'normal conditions under which human cooperation is both possible and necessary'. Society is 'a cooperative venture for mutual advantage' (a view implied but not explicitly stated by Hume) in which 'principles are needed for choosing amongst the various social arrangements which determine the division of advantages and for underwriting an agreement on the proper distributive shares'.[13]

For Rawls, the objective conditions of justice are that many individuals coexist on definite geographical territory, and are sufficiently equal that no one can dominate the rest; all are potentially vulnerable to attack, and each can have plans frustrated by the others; and there is, following Hume, moderate scarcity—goods are not so abundant that cooperation is superfluous, nor so harsh that cooperation is impossible. In summary, the 'circumstances of justice obtain whenever mutually disinterested persons put forward conflicting claims to the division of social advantages under conditions of moderate scarcity.' Without these circumstances, 'there would be no occasion for the virtue of justice, just as in the absence of threats of injury ... there would be no occasion for physical courage'.[14]

Like Hume's, Rawls's account of the circumstances of justice presupposes equality, scarcity, and competition. However, Hume's principles of justice are emergent properties of the circumstances of justice, whereas in Rawls there is, at least ostensibly, no such progression, but rather three discontinuous states: (1) the circumstances of justice (i.e., the real-world conditions under which justice becomes relevant); (2) the original position (the thought experiment which allows us to generate the principles of justice); and (3) the hypothetical well-ordered society that results from them. Critics do not always successfully differentiate between them, and sometimes attribute the more stringent conditions of the original position to the circumstances of justice.[15] Nevertheless, there are striking continuities between them in that all involve social cooperation amongst rationally self-interested equals for reciprocal advantage, thus effectively replicating the conditions (and restrictions) of Hume's circumstances of justice.[16]

THE CIRCUMSTANCES COMPARED

It is clear that although the circumstances of justice and the circumstances of mercy both represent situations in which human beings might find themselves, different types of actors and different types of agency are involved in each case. In the circumstances of justice, people act solely in relation to their interests and (in Rawls's case) their conceptions of the good. They are all assumed to be competent social actors capable of playing multiple and concurrent societal roles who have the ability to assess their options, make rational choices, and (in Rawls's case) negotiate contract terms.[17] It does not actually make much difference to the circumstances of justice whether those involved are embodied or not, in that other entities, corporations, etc., might also be said to have interests and conceptions of the good. In the circumstances of mercy there are always living beings (not necessarily even human) that are capable of being harmed—not just in the sense that some outcome might be contrary to their interests, but that physical injury and death could result.

In both sets of circumstances, the relationship between the parties shapes the potential outcomes. Hume distinguishes goods of the mind, goods of the body, and goods of possession, and both he and Rawls assume that the purpose of society as a whole is the just distribution of these possessions in the face of the conflicting claims of interested parties. The circumstances of mercy, by contrast, are circumstances in which the goods of mind and body are also in question. Yet they are not so much under discussion as under threat. Everyone in the circumstances of justice has a similar motivation—self-interest. In the circumstances of mercy those in need of mercy seek only to survive unharmed, while those who grant mercy may have any motivation or none.[18] So, whereas only one type of agent is needed for the circumstances of justice, the circumstances of mercy necessarily posit two. The circumstances of justice assume approximate equality, whereas the circumstances of mercy are always circumstances of inequality (even if this inequality is a function of time). It can be taken for granted that someone is dominating someone else, or that they have the power to do so.

It is equality that permits reciprocity between the parties, in that (as Hume argues) it is only on the basis of equality that those involved have any incentive to seek it. The idea of reciprocity is also foundational for Rawls. He takes over from Hume the idea that the circumstances of justice involve equals seeking mutual advantage, and he builds reciprocity into the theory itself by arguing that the original position generates a mutually binding agreement that embodies the ideal of reciprocity. It is 'by giving justice to those who can give justice in return [that] the principle of reciprocity is fulfilled'.[19] In the circumstances of mercy, however, reciprocity is impossible. By definition, mercy cannot be given to those who can give mercy in return. Some are at the mercy of all, others have power over many, and it is only in highly artificial situations that anyone can be said simultaneously to have power over and be vulnerable to the same person. (Even in a duel the symmetry only lasts until the first shot is fired.) This breaks with the assumption that everyone has equivalent rights and duties: some have a lot more opportunity to show mercy than others and some have a lot more need of it from a lot more people. For this reason, though the circumstances of mercy are ubiquitous, agents of mercy may be few.

Mercy seems to be applicable in many cases in which justice is not, and, in comparison, the circumstances of justice appear restrictive. If we are to exclude extreme economic necessity, war, and total dependency, it is easy to see that justice has no place in most societies, given that, historically, most have existed with constant war, with at least part of the population at starvation levels, and with the near total economic dependence of women on men, as well as of slaves on their owners. Indeed, it is possible to imagine a world in which the external conditions of Hume's circumstances of justice *never* arise at the same time: one in which there is sometimes abundance without benevolence (e.g., free use of natural resources); sometimes necessity with benevolence (communism/sharing); sometimes necessity without benevolence (famine); sometimes abundance with benevolence (universal charity); and sometimes a combination of these, without there ever being a moderate lack of resources and of benevolence at the same time.

If the circumstances of justice do not include all, or even many, of the circumstances in which people might find themselves, is there perhaps some alternative way of thinking about justice that would be more adequate to our experience? The most promising attempt is offered by Amartya Sen, who has sought to provide an account of justice that is more inclusive than that offered by Rawls.[20] According to Sen, the adequacy of a theory of justice can be measured in terms of its response to the experience of injustice rooted in actual situations. By this measure, Rawls's account fails, because by offering an ideal theory of justice, he provides no comparative measure of justice which would allow us to determine whether one injustice is worse than another. In place of Rawls's model of fair negotiation between interested parties, Sen advocates fair arbitration, which involves becoming the impartial spectators of own motives and actions, and attempting, as Adam Smith put it, 'to view them with the eyes of other people, or as other people are likely to view them'.[21] So, whereas Rawls's theory assumes a closed society, Sen follows Smith in arguing for an open rather than a closed impartiality in which the viewpoints of outsiders who have different perspectives, or who may be affected by the consequences of a decision, are also taken into account.

For Sen the circumstances of justice are above all the circumstances of injustice, the realisation that 'there are clearly remediable injustices around us which we want to eliminate'.[22] His is therefore an approach in which note must be taken of lives blighted by avoidable differences between potential capabilities and actual outcomes. By definition a victim of injustice is a person who suffers as a result of someone else's action or inaction—i.e., as a result of someone else's agency. And, as Sen observes, such injustices can often be related to structurally mediated differentials in power 'to divisions of class, gender, rank, location, religion, community', etc.[23] This means that the circumstances of injustice are not symmetrical and reciprocal (as they are for Rawls's and Hume's circumstances of justice) but rather asymmetrical and nonreciprocal, just as in Hume's thought experiment, in which humans intermingle with a species of creatures possessed of inferior strength.

That Sen's circumstances of justice turn out to be more like the circumstances of mercy is unsurprising, given that it was Judith Shklar's account of injustice that prompted Sen's contention that it is 'the identification of redressable injustice ... [that] animates us to think about justice and injustice'.[24] Believing that cruelty is always unjust, Shklar subsumed her earlier concern to put cruelty first into what she thought of as the more inclusive category of injustice.[25] But if, as Hume contends, there is no question of justice/injustice where power is asymmetrically distributed, then it is cruelty and not injustice that is the true universal. And if that is the case, Sen's attempt to expand the horizons of justice into the circumstances of injustice ends up pointing back to mercy.[26]

CONVENTIONS

Hume might retort that we cannot be in the circumstances of mercy because we do have society and only the justice emerging from the circumstances of justice can ever account for it. As he explains in the *Treatise*, not only is justice 'absolutely necessary' for the wellbeing of mankind, but without it society will fall apart

and everyone will return to a 'savage and solitary condition'. Hume locates the difference between the state
of nature and the human society in settled property
rights, without which human selfishness leads to constant conflict and there can be no peace. In order to
leave 'every one in the peaceable enjoyment of what he
may acquire by his fortune and industry' there needs
to be 'a convention enter'd into by all the members
of the society to bestow stability on the possession of
those external goods'. That convention is justice.[27]

A convention is not the same as a contract, and
Hume emphasises that no formal agreement is required.
The argument goes like this. It is difficult to reach
agreement about property rights because people's self-
interest and acquisitiveness are so strong. There is 'no
passion, therefore, capable of controlling the interested affection, but the very affection itself, by an alteration of its direction'. An accord can therefore only be
reached in the following way:

> I observe, that it will be for my interest to leave
> another in the possession of his goods, provided
> he will act in the same manner with regard to
> me. He is sensible of a like interest in the regu-
> lation of his conduct. When this common sense
> of interest is mutually express'd, and is known
> to both, it produces a suitable resolution and
> behaviour. And this may properly enough be
> call'd a convention or agreement betwixt us, tho'

without the interposition of a promise; since the actions of each of us have a reference to those of the other, and are perform'd upon the supposition, that something is to be perform'd on the other part. Two men, who pull the oars of a boat, do it by an agreement or convention, tho' they have never given promises to each other.... In like manner are languages gradually establish'd by human conventions without any promise. In like manner do gold and silver become the common measures of exchange, and are esteem'd sufficient payment for what is of a hundred times their value.[28]

On this view, justice is not a natural virtue, like the general uncultivated ideas of morality that conform themselves to the partiality of our affections (e.g., self-love, preference for family, etc.). It is, rather, an 'artificial virtue', and only after it is established can there be any conception of justice or injustice at all. Justice is the individual virtue of following these conventional rules. Acceptance of the rules for their utility value represents a distinct second phase: 'Self-interest is the original motive to the establishment of justice: but a sympathy with public interest is the source of the moral approbation, which attends that virtue'.[29] Utility is the sole origin of justice, and reflection on its beneficial consequences the sole foundation of its merit.

This makes justice very different to natural virtues, which are derived from the benevolent passions and take little account of the actions of others or their consequences. The beneficiaries of justice are not necessarily the individuals to whom particular acts are directed (as is the case with acts of charity, or, indeed, mercy) but rather the whole of society, and one-off justice does not even necessarily count as a virtue, and may in itself be 'contrary to the public good'.[30] In the *Enquiry* Hume illustrates the difference as follows:

> The happiness and prosperity of mankind, arising from the social virtue of benevolence and its subdivisions, may be compared to a wall, built by many hands; which still rises by each stone, that is heaped upon it, and receives increase proportional to the diligence and care of each workman. The same happiness, raised by the social virtue of justice and its subdivisions, may be compared to the building of a vault, where each individual stone would, of itself, fall to the ground; nor is the whole fabric supported but by the mutual assistance and combination of its corresponding parts.[31]

The conventions of justice are like a vault because each individual relies on every other, and the whole structure stands or falls in its entirety. For that reason 'every man, in embracing that virtue, must have an eye on the whole plan or system, and must expect the concurrence of his fellows in the same conduct and behaviour'.[32] There are two corollaries of this all-or-nothing argument: the first is that individual acts of natural virtue do not contribute to society at all (only to individuals within it); the second is that every aberration from conventional norms threatens the entire fabric of society, with 'disorder and confusion' following upon 'every breach of these rules'.[33]

Where, then, does this leave mercy? Hume's argument implies that mercy, like any other form of humanity or benevolence, cannot produce an equivalent outcome, because it is not joined up. No matter how many soldiers fail to shoot the people they come across in ditches, it can never add up to anything that could be called society. Justice comes as a package in a way that benevolence does not. And the reason it is an all-or-nothing package is that it is conventional. Everyone has to join in for it to work at all. So, what appears to be its weakness, its artificiality, is actually its strength: if it exists, it is also comprehensive.

All this can sound suspiciously circular: society is a collection of persons amongst whom justice obtains, so justice is the only way to produce it. But if the claim is meant to be more than definitional, then it is susceptible to disconfirmation. And if by society Hume means anything that is recognisably a stable form of sociability involving human beings, then to disprove this hypothesis all that is necessary is to show that such sociability is possible without justice, and that (contrary to Hume's claim of all or nothing) it continues in the breach. This requires a demonstration not just that mercy or benevolence is possible without justice, but that it constitutes something like society.

Many, probably most, forms of sociability rely upon conventions, but it does not follow that all forms of sociability are conventional or that sociability itself is a convention. It is clear that some forms of sociability are more conventional than others, and some sociability appears not to be conventional at all. In the *Enquiry* Hume concedes that the conventions of justice would not arise in a state of war or a golden age of abundance, universal good or ill-will, or necessity. Perhaps none of these scenarios provides an immediately credible account of sociability, but Hume also offers several hypothetical accounts of sociability outside society (as defined by the convention of justice): the wall of benevolence; the sociability exemplified by the gentle usage of inferiors; and the family formed by natural affection (which he claims is the basic building block of society).[34]

Hume may claim that 'without justice society must immediately dissolve', but were there 'a species of creatures intermingled with men', to whom justice would not apply but to whom 'we should be bound by the laws of humanity to give gentle usage', the result would be a form of sociability. Hume is consistent in that he claims that 'our intercourse with them could not be called society', but it is nevertheless not the 'savage and solitary condition' of the state of nature either.[35] What is it? Conventions of justice are not needed in situations of such inequality, and yet some form of sociability would seem to be possible. If so, it would presumably be like the wall of benevolence: 'a wall, built by many hands', certainly, but one which is the aggregation of individual acts of benevolence, and so 'rises by each stone'. Gentle usage is a form of benevolence, and so the sociability of gentle usage and the wall of benevolence are created the same way—through an accumulation of one-shot interactions. As such, neither presupposes a set of shared conventions, and the nature of the aggregation is a function of the individual acts that compose it ('proportional to the diligence and care of each workman'), not a characteristic of the whole.

RADICAL SOCIABILITY

One way to think about this possibility in a more systematic way is through Hume's own analogy with language. Hume's account of the role of convention in the origins of justice inspired David K. Lewis's discussion of convention in language, to which Donald Davidson's anticonventionalism is a response.[36] To what extent might a version of Davidson's arguments about language be applicable to Hume's account of society? According to Hume, society (peace) requires security of property, which, given human selfishness, can arise only through convention. Similarly, language requires stability of meaning, which can arise and be secured only through convention. Is there an analogy to be made with Donald Davidson's argument that convention is neither a necessary nor a sufficient condition of successful communication?

Davidson offers two kinds of examples to demonstrate the point. The first involves radical interpretation —i.e., interpreting the meanings of a speaker's utterances 'from scratch'—and the other the interpretation of linguistic errors such as malapropism. Radical interpretation involves creating a theory of interpretation in the absence of any knowledge of the speaker's vocabulary or beliefs, or the conventions governing interpretation in their language. We might imagine this taking place in first-contact situations, across time, between species, or whatever (situations not unlike Hume's hypothetical examples of gentle usage). The thought experiment involves an interpreter, a speaker, and the possibility of interpreting or misinterpreting the speaker's utterance. The basic situation is asymmetrical and nonreciprocal (speakers are at the mercy of their interpreters when it comes to making themselves understood), and the possible outcomes range from perfect understanding to total incomprehension. In these circumstances, what would make interpretation possible? Davidson calls it the 'principle of charity' or the 'principle of rational accommodation', and argues that it involves 'assigning truth conditions to alien sentences that make native speakers right when plausibly possible, according, of course, to our own view of what is right'.[37]

The principle of charity is justified by the inadmissibility of too many absurd beliefs: 'the fact that we can dismiss a priori the chance of massive error'.[38] A theory of interpretation must be wrong if it ends up making most of the speaker's beliefs untrue, because there's a limit to how wrong you can be about something and still be taken to be talking about it. The principle of charity supposes that an interpretation is better (i.e., enhances understanding) if it leads to attributing more true beliefs. For this reason, 'I can interpret your words correctly only by interpreting so as to put us largely in agreement'.[39] Maximizing agreement between speaker and interpreter therefore requires the interpreter to suppress scepticism about the speaker's beliefs, because no communication can take place unless people generally abstain from disbelieving each other.

Hume argues that the conventions of justice that erect the vault of society are like those that create the web of language. But if language itself is not necessarily conventional, maybe society is not, either. Perhaps a radical sociability is possible? Radical sociability would involve sociability without the constraints of, or even reliance on, preexisting social rules, codes, or agreements. That's clear enough. But what are the criteria of sociability? That's a difficult question, like asking what counts as communication. But just as communication boils down to interpreting someone else's semantic intentions without misunderstanding them, sociability involves interacting without harming them, because otherwise it is not sociability but war. If such interaction requires one-off, nonreciprocal benevolence, then it counts as radical sociability.

What might be called a 'principle of mercy' would involve imposing constraints on your own actions to maximize sociability between self and others. You would have to follow it most of the time, because otherwise there could be no sociability. There's a limit to how much harm you can do to someone while still being sociable. We might want to discuss what the minimum threshold is for contact and what the maximum level for harm, but it is clear that such thresholds exist: fights to the death and total solitude are never sociable. However, very little contact need be involved. If someone throws a stone at random off a cliff, that doesn't count as sociability because it is solitary, and if it hits someone on the beach below that is not sociable either; it is harm (whether intended or not). But if they throw it so as to avoid hitting someone on the beach, that is sociable, because there is at least potential contact and minimised harm. Windowless monads are never sociable, however perfect their harmony, but two individuals with some implicit awareness of each other and the potential for contact would count as such: for example, two strangers who unconsciously avoid bumping into each other in the street. Of course, rules and conventions do exist. The example of two people avoiding bumping into each other provides a good example: having a convention to 'keep to the left' is going to be more secure than depending on individual examples of one-shot benevolence, but one-shot benevolence will do. If they have the grace to do so, two people can avoid bumping into each other, even if they have never met before and do not know the rules of the road.

How might this process work to create society? Going back to the Diamond example, let's suppose that a territory is made up of adjoining cells like a honeycomb, and let us assume that the circumstances of mercy hold throughout. Each cell is inhabited by people strong enough to kill any outsider who enters it, and if someone strays from their own cell into an adjacent one, they are immediately despatched. The contiguity of the cells notwithstanding, it could not be said that the people living within them collectively constituted a society or (supposing that they were not in virtual contact) that any form of sociability existed between them. But if, in some cases, people were permitted to cross over into an adjacent cell (irrespective of whether the concession was made reciprocally), some degree of sociability would be possible within the territory, notwithstanding the fact that there might be some cells no one could enter without being killed, and that no concession of free passage was reciprocal. People could have some contact with one another without violence or fear, and that is sociability. The cells involved might not all join up, but where they were contiguous with one another they might justifiably be thought to constitute something approximating a society, notwithstanding the fact that free movement in every direction was impossible, and that some cells within the territory were excluded.

Imagine that each cell where movement is possible from at least one direction is replaced by a stone, and you have what Hume describes as a wall of benevolence: 'a wall, built by many hands; which still rises by each stone, that is heaped upon it, and receives encrease proportional to the diligence and care of each workman'.[40] Mercy provides one way of describing how such a structure might take shape without the inhabitants of one cell reaching agreement with another. Some people treat trespasses mercifully, and even if everyone does so independently of everyone else, the outcome is still free movement between some of the cells. But it all depends on individual acts of mercy and not at all on their coordination.

Could a structure made this way hold up like a vault? Davidson's second type of example is relevant here; it involves the misuse of language, which presents less of an obstacle to communication than the conventionalist theory would suggest. The argument is that if, for example, we allow that a malapropism might count as an example of successful linguistic communication, then it cannot be claimed that conventional meaning is essential to communication: 'Knowledge of the conventions of language is thus a practical crutch to interpretation', but one we 'could in theory have done without from the start'.[41] All that is needed to enable communication in such cases is a 'passing theory', not the 'prior theory' based in existing conventions. To interpret a malapropism the interpreter has to set aside the prior theory they had been planning to use, and come up with and use an ad hoc theory that makes better sense of the speaker's utterance.[42] For example, when Mrs Malaprop advises someone to 'illiterate him quite from your memory', our ability to interpret the sentence correctly depends not on any shared prior theory about the meaning of 'illiterate', but one that we have to make up then and there in the hope that it coincides with Mrs Malaprop's theory.

A malapropism is communicative if the interpreter departs from the standard conventions of interpretation so as to minimise the potential for misunderstanding with the speaker and maximise communication. In this respect, the charitable interpretation of a malapropism is like an act of mercy that departs from an existing norm, such as that of justice, in order to do less harm. For example, let us suppose that, as Hume claims, justice is a set of conventions about property that enable interested parties not to fight over it, and that there is a merciful departure from the norms of justice—e.g., someone steals a sheep but is allowed to go unpunished rather than be transported to Australia. On Hume's account, that should undermine the stability of the entire edifice of justice, or at the very least start to turn those in society away from sociability and towards savagery. But that is not necessarily the case. It is by no means unreasonable to imagine that mercy might enhance rather than diminish trust and social solidarity. If anything, acts of mercy are generally taken to be prosocial: by acknowledging the fragility of the weak, the strong recognise their shared humanity, and the weak have less reason to resent their position. Indeed, as Hay argues in the case of Hume's own society, enhanced social solidarity was the motivation for mercy, or, if not that, its latent function.

The idea that you might be able to remove a stone from the vault of justice and leave a hole without causing total collapse might seem like a modest claim. And yet it is not one we should take for granted, for if mercy is a breach of convention that enhances sociability or leaves sociability unchanged, then that disproves the theory that the conventions of justice are necessary for society. If a one-off departure from those conventions is just as, or perhaps even more, effective in bringing about the same result, then it is clear that the conventions of justice are something that we can sometimes do without. And if we can do without them sometimes, then it is reasonable to ask how much of the time we can operate without them, or whether we need them at all. The implications of this are far-reaching. If radical sociability is possible, then the conventional account of society is not necessarily true. As Davidson argues, if linguistic ability is just 'the ability to converge on a passing theory from time to time ... we have erased the boundary between knowing a language and knowing our way around in the world generally'.[43] By the same measure, if sociability is ever just the capacity for mercy, then we have abandoned the idea of society as something wholly distinct from a sociable anarchy.

This argument points the way back to the shadow side of early modern theories of human sociability, and suggests that Hume's thought experiment about 'gentle usage' might be a viable alternative to theories of society based on justice (whether through contract or convention). Accounts of society based on contract or convention presuppose an all-or-nothing dichotomy: either you are in society or in the state of nature, at peace or at war. But even with lots of conventions and contracts woven into it, social life as a whole does not have to be conventional or contractual. Just as communication seems to be possible both without conventions (radical interpretation) and in the breach of them (malapropism), sociability encompasses both unfinished societies and their decaying ruins, and any theory of society needs to be able to account for both the emergence and the fragile survival of those structures.

It is easy to see the underlying similarity between communication and sociability: they are what allow humans and other animals to be together rather than alone. Both depend on what are essentially nonreciprocal relationships (albeit ones that allow for frequent alternation): between the interpreter and the interpreted, and between the powerful and those whom they have power over. Furthermore, one is usually impossible without the other.

Suppose a soldier comes across someone stuck in a bog. The soldier is someone who routinely performs any favour asked of her. But in this case they have no common language, and although the person in the bog keeps making gestures, the soldier does not know for certain what they mean, and concludes that there is no way of guessing, because as far as she knows, they could mean anything whatsoever. So she leaves them where they are. The harm here lies not in the failure to perform an act of charity (because that is something the soldier would automatically do if she realised that was what was required) but in the absence of charitable interpretation. Indeed, the refusal of charitable interpretation counts as harm in and of itself, for someone who is never interpreted charitably experiences social death.

The problem with Hume's and Rawls's theories of justice is that they presuppose a sphere of sociability much narrower than the one we actually experience. Mercy provides a better account of the way society is, in the sense that it allows society to be the shape and size that we experience it to be (i.e., shapeless and indeterminate). Of course, the principle of mercy is not a principle at all, any more than Hume's laws of humanity are really laws. But something like it is needed to explain the successfully improvisational nature of sociability—the fact that (in human behaviour as much or more than in language) we are forever making things up as we go along, and that this can be enough even when the stakes are high.

For communication and sociability to be possible, the interpreters and the powerful have only to minimise scepticism and harm. And given that communication and sociability are possible, then it is fair to assume that this is what is happening most of the time. Rawls's claim that 'justice is the first virtue of social institutions, as truth is of systems of thought' might be restated as 'mercy is the precondition of sociability, as charitable interpretation is of communication'.[44] It is up to the proponents of justice to show that something other than mercy is needed to explain our day-to-day survival.

3

Suppose that some form of human society exists on the basis of radical sociability; from one moment to the next, the stronger allow the weaker to go about their business, and take no advantage of momentary or even enduring powerlessness. The circumstances of mercy are more or less universal, and so too is the principle of mercy, thanks to which individuals are routinely able to have contact with others and yet survive unharmed. As a result of the diffusion of mercy, in some places the circumstances of mercy give rise to the circumstances of justice. In this situation, relatively free and equal individuals come to or choose to regulate their dealings through some set of implicitly agreed conventions or mutually agreed rules appropriate to their objectives; clubs, corporations, companies, online communities, card schools, communes—perhaps even states could result. Where this happens there are islands of justice within the wider sea of mercy whose internal norms are potentially at odds with those outside. What happens then? Is mercy just the precursor of virtue? Can justice supersede mercy and exclude it entirely, as political theorists imagine happening in the transition from the state of nature to the social state? Or do the two virtues somehow coexist?

In these circumstances, the relationship of justice to mercy is akin to that envisaged by the medieval theologians who describe divine justice operating in a world sustained by God's mercy. If the fact of existence rather than nonexistence is, for every creature, attributable to God's mercy, then divine justice must always presuppose it.[1] However, if God's mercy is comprehensive, it does not only mean refraining from the annihilation of his creatures, but practising mercy in all his dealings with them, including the norms of justice he has established. So, if divine justice coexists with mercy, how do the two relate? Anselm was the first to explore the paradoxes involved in a systematic way: (1) how can it be just for God, in his mercy, to save the wicked, and (2) why, if it is just to save the wicked, are some to be saved and others not? These two questions have never gone away, and variants of them shape this chapter: Is mercy compatible with justice? And, if mercy is allowable, how inclusive must it be?[2]

Although it is easy to see that justice is compatible with doing less harm than you might, it is not obviously compatible with doing less than the norm suggests where that norm is itself just. Where there is no existing norm for justice, a merciful act might well turn out to be identical to what was later established to be just in the same circumstances. And where the norm exceeded by mercy is not a norm prescribed by justice, mercy and justice may coincide as well. But what about the norms of justice itself: Would it not be merciful to exceed those as well? This is where Anselm's paradox kicks in. In modern secular form it can be stated as follows: 'If mercy requires a tempering of justice, then there is a sense in which mercy may require a departure from justice.... Thus to be merciful is perhaps to be unjust. But it is a vice, not a virtue, to manifest injustice. Thus mercy must be, not a virtue, but a vice'. On the other hand, Jeffrie Murphy continues, if mercy refers merely to the requirement that the penalty fit the particular circumstances of the crime, then it is no longer 'an autonomous virtue and instead becomes a part of ... justice'. So 'mercy either is a vice or is redundant'.[3]

There are several possible responses to this paradox, but they serve chiefly to show how difficult a problem it really is. Murphy himself argues that mercy is confined to private as opposed to public law, and that there is a paradox only in a 'criminal law paradigm' (e.g., *Measure for Measure*, where Isabella pleads for mercy for her brother Claudio, awaiting execution under the law); in the 'private law paradigm' (e.g., *The Merchant of Venice*, where Portia defends Antonio, who has defaulted on his contract with Shylock), mercy only involves waiving a right that could be justly claimed rather than violating an obligation. Anselm's paradox might perhaps be resolved in this way (supposing a God who is not bound by his own rules), but allowing that mercy can be exercised only in a private context basically concedes its incompatibility with justice as a public norm.[4]

Alternatively, perhaps mercy can be reconciled with justice if we think of mercy as involving the selection of one of the milder alternatives from within a range of just punishments. For example, if someone deserves to be rewarded for good service, there is more than one form that reward can take. If the converse is also true, then for any crime there might be a 'disjunction of penalties' equally just but varying in their severity (e.g., from a fine to a custodial sentence). In these circumstances, mercy might be served by imposing one of the less severe of the options.[5] However, if two states of affairs are equivalent in their appropriateness as penalties, it is hard to see why they would not be roughly equivalent in their severity (mitigating circumstances having been taken into account), given that this is the normal basis on which crimes and penalties are matched. In which case, mercy seems redundant as a way of describing the choice between them, for the concept of mercy, if it is applicable at all, applies not to such marginal cases, but to those where someone receives a lighter penalty than they deserve.

Ned Markosian takes a different approach. He argues that mercy is always relative to something, and so distinguishes different forms of argument about mercy in terms of the option to which the merciful option is preferred. On this 'flexible' analysis, an action is both merciful and permissible if both alternatives are permissible under the same notion of permissibility (which might include prudence, justice, legality, morality, or whatever). This response has the great benefit of acknowledging (like the normative one) that the criterion against which a merciful act is defined is not going to be of a single kind. However, this means that the solution to Anselm's first paradox depends on the form of permissibility involved, and, while there might be no conflict under other notions of permissibility, the justice analysis of mercy 'leaves us with no way of resolving Anselm's puzzle about justice and mercy. For if it would have been just for x to perform B, and if B is worse for y than A, then it is hard to see how it could be just for x to perform A'.[6]

This suggests that it will be very hard to resolve Anselm's paradox without changing the terms in which it is formulated. But while it may be legitimate to argue that justice is not the only virtue, and that virtues sometimes conflict, the idea that it may be unjust but not immoral to prefer mercy sidesteps rather than resolves Anselm's dilemma.[7] A superficially more promising approach is to argue that justice itself is a complex concept and that retributive justice is a means to an end that might in some cases be better served if retribution were tempered by mercy. On this view, retributive norms must be guided by the communicative point of the law. Whatever the grounds for mercy (the offender's personal history, repentance, etc.) this would not mean any adjustment to the punishment judged to be merited—rather, merely acknowledging 'that the imposition of the sentence warranted by the retributive norm is an excessive hardship'.[8] This is a clever response, because it tries to divide the concept of justice in two and transform mercy into the link between them (a role usually assigned to equity). Yet if the punishment judged to be deserved remains unchanged, then someone who does not receive mercy has good grounds for claiming that they have been treated unjustly compared to someone who has.

If mercy is always going to be unjust where justice is normative, then justice can only function when mercy is excluded. Where justice is operative it must therefore be an autonomous social practice, quite independent of mercy, effectively transcending its origins and superimposing a set of principles in which mercy plays no part. Is that possible?

EQUITY

Maybe, for a time, but it is not straightforward, as Aristotle was the first to note. When applied to the complex realities of human social life (rather than the ideal circumstances of justice), the principles of justice often seem to need to be adjusted to fit the facts, to avoid becoming unjust instead. Aristotle calls this adjustment equity, *epieikeia*. As he presents it in the *Nicomachean Ethics*, this process is internal to justice and concerns the relationship between universal justice (i.e., 'anything that tends to produce or conserve the happiness ... of a political association') which is 'complete virtue', and particular justice, which is merely a part of virtue and refers to the fulfilment of the requirements of the law with regard to both the distribution and rectification of goods and retributive justice.[9] Although particular justice is part of universal justice, there are occasions on which particular justice may be at odds with universal justice and universal justice is aligned with something else, namely equity.

Just as an architect would not measure a fluted column with a straight edge, but rather with the leaden rule of the Lesbians, which could be bent to fit any shape, so equity is a rule that fits the specific case. According to Aristotle, *epieikeia* involves a 'rectification of legal justice' that is in line with universal justice, 'a ruling such as the legislator himself would have given if he had been present'. Equity is, therefore, better than any kind of particular justice, but not 'better than absolute justice'. From this, Aristotle draws the following controversial conclusion: the equitable person is someone 'who is not unduly insistent on his rights, but accepts less than his share, although he has the law on his side'.[10]

In the *Rhetoric* Aristotle turns to equity again. It is, he suggests, part of the unwritten law; rather than being outside the law altogether (like the virtues of generosity, or gratitude, or courage, etc.), it is specifically designed to make up 'for the defects of a community's written code of law'. From this definition, it is plain what sort of actions, and what sort of persons, are equitable or the reverse:

> Equity bids us be merciful to the weakness of human nature; to think less about the laws than about the man who framed them, and less about what he said than about what he meant; not to consider the actions of the accused so much as his intentions, nor this or that detail so much as the whole story; to ask not what a man is now but what he has always or usually been.[11]

Aristotle consistently implies that equity inclines to leniency. But it is not immediately obvious why this should be so. After all, should equity not require greater severity as often as leniency? But if it is the case that equity inclines to mercy, then this raises questions about what sort of concept equity really is, and, ultimately, whether it can be contained within the conceptual framework of justice at all.

As Martha Nussbaum notes, the puzzle of equity is 'the unexplained connection between appropriate situational judgement and mercy'. Rather than allowing that such judgements might go either way, Greek and Roman thinkers seem to think that 'the decision to concern oneself with particulars is connected with taking up a gentle and lenient cast of mind toward human wrongdoing'. Her explanation is that ancient Greek justice was already as harsh as it could be. Crimes had to be avenged symmetrically and in full, even if the original perpetrator were dead. But considered in terms of individual culpability, things become more complicated. Is it, for example, appropriate to punish Oedipus as a parricide when he could not know that the man he killed was his father? Thinking this way, as a spectator of Greek tragedy is invited to do, an asymmetry emerges. Justice may demand a full, symmetrical penalty, but 'the particulars of the case, more closely inspected, lead toward extenuation or mitigation far more frequently than in the opposite direction'. Someone who interprets a complex legal case as a reader interprets a story, or a spectator a drama, inevitably encounters 'two features of the equitable: its attentiveness to particularity and its capacity for sympathetic understanding'. If they interpret well they are 'already prepared for equity and, in turn, for mercy'.[12]

However, there may be more to it than that, especially in a modern context. As John Tasioulas argues, the asymmetry of equity is a broader phenomenon which cannot fully be explained by Nussbaum's account. To explain this it is necessary to look beyond the vicissitudes and complexities of human life (which may or may not be present as mitigating factors) to the nature of legality itself. Even supposing it to be consistent with justice, the 'discretionary aggravation' of the 'strict requirements of criminal law' would be a violation of 'the principle that criminal liability and sanctions should be imposed in accordance with clear and determinate laws declared in advance to those subject to them (*nulla poena sine lege*)'.[13] This raises the possibility (which he elsewhere rejects) that mercy is less a concession to human frailty than 'a by-product of the asymmetry of mitigation and aggravation consequent on the interplay between equity and legality'.[14]

These explanations are not mutually exclusive. One potential route to mercy is the interplay of equity and precedent through which equitable judgements are incorporated into the law. An equitable judgement will itself set a precedent (we would not want inequitable judgements to be precedents), and so if equity is applied asymmetrically, judgements will necessarily become progressively more merciful, making the law itself more merciful while not exhausting the scope for further discretion in the future. Nussbaum herself argues that 'the dialogue between rule and perception in Aristotelian morality' is like that of a judge who sees her decisions 'as parts of a concrete history, evolving through ... the complex interaction of principle, precedent, and new perception'.[15] This process, which some have likened to the writing of a chain novel, amounts to rather more than filling in gaps in the law or 'putting law into the condition to which it aspires in the first place'.[16] It is not something that happens once, rectifying an omission or anomaly once and for all.

Given that the need for equity arises from the application of justice to particular individuals in novel, complex, or ambiguous circumstances, it is, by definition, always a work in progress. Closing up one gap is liable to open up another and clarifying one anomaly may put other, previously unambiguous cases into question.

This has far-reaching implications for the argument about whether justice can be both self-sufficient and sustainable without reference to mercy. If justice requires equity, and equity consistently errs on the side of mercy, this suggests not only that equity both embodies mercy relative to particular justice, but that it will incrementally move universal justice in a more merciful direction. Nussbaum rejects this conclusion: 'It seems wrong to make a simple contrast between justice and equity ... it is justice itself, not a departure from justice, to use equity's flexible standard'.[17] That's a reassuring idea, but it is not sustainable. Equity, in Aristotle's sense, is by definition always a departure from the fixed norm of particular justice. But the universal justice with which equity aligns the particular is not itself a different fixed norm to which equity returns time and again, but a developing consensus about what sort of judgements are conducive to the common good of a particular polity. It is equity itself that reveals to us what universal justice requires. And if equity is a way of reading evidence through sympathetic understanding that enlarges the potential for merciful discretion, this too will contribute to that developing consensus.

Equity transforms justice into something more merciful both through its incorporation into law through asymmetrical precedent, and through its establishing the pattern that universal justice always inclines to mercy, which carries the implication not only that the scope for mercy can be extended, but that such universal justice is in practice indistinguishable from it.

Where does this leave the idea (with which this chapter began) that there might be spheres of justice within the wider circumstances of mercy? If justice requires equity, which leads to mercy, the distinction between justice and mercy will be undermined. Suppose that a social space exists in which we have the Humean circumstances of justice, and that a set of principles is established with rules for the division of property and a system of forfeitures for those who infringe them. In the surrounding area there are marked inequalities, order is maintained through gentle usage, and goods are apportioned on this basis as well. Within the sphere of justice, forfeitures will be progressively reduced or not required, with the result that the difference between the treatment of those who have infringed the rules and those who have followed them gradually diminishes. In these circumstances, the rules, not being enforced, gradually cease to be effective, with the consequence that the principles of justice no longer hold, having been replaced by leniency.

This is a very different outcome to the one envisaged by Nussbaum in *Frontiers of Justice*. The underlying situation is similar in that she is concerned with the relationship between those included and those excluded from the sphere of justice (in this case the Rawlsian one). The latter—the disabled, nonnationals, and other species—are like Hume's 'creatures of inferior strength' in that there is 'a serious asymmetry of power and capacity' between the dominant group by whom the principles of justice are framed and those affected by their actions. However, believing Rawls's theory of justice to be 'the strongest theory of political justice we have', she claims that it should not be replaced but extended.[18] Nussbaum sees the capabilities approach as the best supplement to Rawls, and argues that, although it is not designed to secure mutual advantage and is outcome-orientated rather than procedural, it nevertheless enhances the range of application of Rawls's intuitive principles of fairness and reciprocity, 'extending justice to all those in the world who ought to be treated justly'. However, as Nussbaum acknowledges, seeking the outcomes of justice without either the circumstances or procedures of justice to rely on 'requires people to have very great sympathy and benevolence, and to sustain these sentiments over time'.[19] But if that is how justice is to be extended to 'creatures of inferior strength', then it is not clear how it differs from mercy or Hume's 'laws of humanity'.

There is therefore an unresolved tension between Nussbaum's endorsement of Aristotle's account of equity and her adherence to Rawls's account of justice.

Many of her arguments both here and elsewhere point to the centrality of mercy rather than justice, but she still maintains that justice remains the key political virtue, and that all that is needed is equity to ensure fairness within the frontiers of justice and the capabilities approach to extend the principles of justice beyond its borders. This leaves a void at the centre of her political thinking. She assumes that the circumstances of justice occupy most of the territory and that justice need only be fairly implemented and more widely applied. But, in fact, things are likely to go the other way. Equity will undermine justice from within and lead to mercy, and the gentle usage required to implement the capabilities approach shows that the procedures of justice are not needed to achieve the outcomes of justice at all. If the circumstances of mercy are more widespread than those of justice, there can be no empire of justice: only porous spheres of justice floating in a sea of mercy.

LEVELLING

All these examples are rather abstract, so let's take a historical example of equity at work. In the early modern period, notions of equity were central to both legal and political thought. And though some allowed that equity might lead to the aggravation of punishment, the underlying supposition was that (in the often quoted words attributed to Saint Cyprian) 'equity is justice tempered with the sweetness of mercy'.[20] In English law this idea found institutional expression in the division between the common law and the court of equity. The former was represented by acts of Parliament and the decisions of the courts; the latter in the Court of Chancery which worked alongside, and sometimes in opposition to, the common law, guided only by the king's conscience. In practice, the Court of Chancery was presided over by the lord chancellor who was, as Cardinal Wolsey put it, 'an officer to execute justice with clemency, where conscience is opposed to the rigour of the law'.[21.]

The understanding that equity might override the common law ensured that appeals to equity were frequently made by both sides in the English Civil War, especially by the radical wing of the Parliamentary cause. Even here it was clear that the notion was used in a way continuous with Aristotle.[22] Yet in the space of a few years, equity was being used to justify wholesale revolution. It was already a legal commonplace that equity represented the spirit rather than the letter of the law, but a Parliamentary broadsheet of 1642 pushed this further: by itself, the law is 'a body without a soul'. It is equity, which need not even be 'expressed in the law', but is rather the natural law 'implied and supposed in all laws' that 'gives life to authority'.[23] At this stage, Parliament was appealing to equity against the legal authority of the king, but radical groups quickly turned the same arguments against Parliament itself.

Writing from Newgate prison in 1647, the Leveller Richard Overton argued that '*the equity of the Law is Superiour to the Letter* ... [and] if the Law should comptroule and overthrow the *equity,* it is to be comptrouled and overthrowne it selfe, and the *equity* to be preserved as the *thing,* only legally, *obligatory and binding*'.[24]

There was seemingly nowhere this argument could not go. For if equity, as natural law, is always to be preferred to the letter of the law, and equity implies mercy, then it would seem to follow that mercy is always to be preferred to the law. The True Levellers, or Diggers, led by Gerrard Winstanley, showed just what this might mean. Proclaiming Christ to be 'the greatest, first and truest Leveller', Winstanley made the distinction between established laws ('the selfish murdering fleshly Lawes of this Nation') and the law of equity into a question of cosmic significance.[25] The triumph of the latter involves a dramatic repudiation of property rights in favour of a primitive communism: 'When this universall law of equity rises up in every man and woman, then none shall lay claim to any creature, and say, *This is mine, and that is yours, This is my work, that is yours*; but every one shall put to their hands to till the earth ... and the blessing of the earth shall be common to all'.[26] Winstanley and his followers soon put this into practice; in 1649, they occupied common land in Surrey and began distributing the produce to all who joined them.

The rapidity with which the Aristotelian idea of equity was transformed from its role as a merciful corrective to common law into a justification for political revolution and the community of goods is astonishing. And it brings us back to Anselm's second paradox. The first hinged on the question of whether mercy was ever compatible with justice; the second explored the question of whether, if mercy is countenanced, it can consistently be shown only to some and not to others. Why, given that God has 'mercy upon all' are all not to be saved?[27] Within the early church, some, notably Origen, thought that they would be, and espoused the doctrine of universal salvation. For a time even Augustine agreed with him. The 'goodness of God' (*Dei bonitas*) means that, unlike royal mercy, divine mercy is unlimited and 'leads all the beings that have fallen until they are restored to the condition from which they have fallen'.[28] Winstanley fused this argument with the Levellers' interpretation of equity, and in his early apocalyptic tracts argued for universal salvation on the basis of God's mercy and goodness.[29] A divine law of equity combines the limitlessness of salvation with the law of equity, and so ensure that property is made available to all who need it, without exception, just as salvation is available to all who need it. Translated into economic terms, universal salvation becomes negative community, for unlimited access to divine mercy can only mean unlimited access to the 'common treasury' of the earth, from which none can be excluded. No wonder people complained that equity was 'a roguish thing'.[30]

But how is such a radical conclusion to be avoided? Modern philosophers argue that Anselm's second paradox is less of a problem than it appears because mercy is an imperfect duty and there is some flexibility in the way it can be fulfilled. Duties are said to be imperfect when, if the duty is to be fulfilled at all, it has to be fulfilled on some occasions and not others. For example, we may feel that we have a duty to help persons in need. But if we as individuals were obliged to help all people in need at all times, we would soon lack the resources to do so.[31] This potentially allows us to clarify the question of whether mercy is (1) merely permissible; (2) perfectly obligatory; (3) imperfectly obligatory; or (4) supererogatory. While mercy is not supererogatory (one is liable to be blamed for never performing acts of mercy and being a merciless person), it nevertheless appears to be an imperfect obligation (in that one cannot be blamed for not acting mercifully in any particular instance). So it is possible to be a merciful person (who performs acts of mercy through compassion or some other motivation) and still not perform a merciful act (defined as less harsh than normal in the circumstances) on some occasion when it is possible to do so.[32]

However, while this might be a serviceable response for individuals who have the opportunity to perform private acts of mercy, it is not clear that it gets to grips with the real issue, which is that some agents may, by definition, have qualities by virtue of which all obligations are perfect. This applies to God in Anselm's paradox: since God is perfectly just, he has what in other circumstances would be called a perfect obligation to act justly, which would seem to exclude mercy altogether. However, if he also has a perfect duty to be good and mercy is entailed by the perfect goodness, then his mercy should be limitless. (A God who is merciful to the wicked as well as to the good is better than one who is merciful only to the good, so, given that God is 'all-good and supremely good', it seems to follow that universal salvation will be best of all.)[33]

The argument could go the other way, of course (which is why it is a paradox), and the same is true in nontheological contexts—for example, if you think that states too have perfect rather than imperfect duties. According to Ross Harrison, states ought to be purely rational entities, and to act rationally is to act justly (i.e., treat like cases in the same way). We might want the state to act mercifully, but 'only by forgoing mercy can we enable the state (or other authority) to behave like a fully rational entity, accountable for all its actions to the people over whom it has power'.[34] Without this there will be 'mere power without accountability', and anything less than unbroken accountability will delegitimate the state. Mercy is therefore incompatible with legitimacy.

This puts the bar rather high: it is surely too strong to claim that the state qua state had such a perfect obligation to be rational or accountable or good. (Not

every legislative anomaly is grounds for revolution.)
The one thing that the state might be thought to have
as a perfect obligation is the obligation not to be cruel.
That is certainly the implication of 'putting cruelty
first' and the 'liberalism of fear'. And it is the wisdom
embedded in the longstanding idea that the people
may overthrow a cruel tyrant, which is why Williams
emphasises that 'a solution to the first political question is required *all the time*'.[35] But there are two ways
to break down the idea of having a perfect obligation
not to be cruel. On the one hand, putting cruelty first
might be taken to mean that mercy will always take
priority, with the result that the state has an obligation to be merciful at all times. On the other, it could
also be argued that the state has a perfect duty not to
be cruel and only an imperfect duty to be merciful.
But even an imperfect duty will have a markedly asymmetrical effect. If you have a perfect obligation never
to be cruel, and a duty to be merciful only some of the
time, then the outcome will, in the long run, be the
same, with the result that it is impossible to separate
the effects of an imperfect duty to be merciful from a
perfect one. Thus, if mercy is countenanced at all, there
is ultimately no reason not to be merciful to everyone.

Let's go back to Anselm's two paradoxes. The first
hinged on the question of whether mercy is compatible with justice, the second on whether mercy can be
shown only selectively. Those who draw the seemingly
inescapable conclusion that (where justice provides the

norms from which mercy departs) mercy is incompatible with justice usually accept that mercy should be excluded from justice. Yet if equity is required for the exercise of justice, and is liable to lead to mercy, then perhaps mercy cannot be entirely excluded from justice after all. And, as Anselm's second paradox indicates, mercy, once allowed, is difficult to stop, because it is by definition a virtue that exceeds any given norm. So, if mercy is incompatible with justice, and yet impossible to eradicate from the practice of justice, then it follows that mercy will ultimately undermine justice altogether. This inevitably raises the question of whether it is worth trying to hold on to justice at all.

Almost all political philosophers would say yes, of course, justice must take priority over anything that stands in its way. But as Raymond Geuss points out, it is unclear that we have what Rawls claims is an 'intuitive conviction of the primacy of justice'.[36] Might it not be possible to do without justice, and rely on mercy instead? One of the few philosophers even to consider the possibility is Nietzsche, who envisions two scenarios in which justice might effectively cease to function: either as the result of the increasing omnipotence of the powerful, or through an acceptance of loss of power.[37] In the latter case, a society 'becomes so pathologically soft and tender that among other things it sides even with those who harm it' because punishment 'somehow seems unfair'.[38] But on what basis might such extreme conclusions ever appear acceptable? They come from liberalism, but even if we allow that a liberalism of fear will eventually lead to a communism of mercy like that of Winstanley's negative community or Nietzsche's society that will not punish, the consequences seem difficult to swallow. For if mercy is incompatible with justice, then putting mercy before justice like this can only mean tolerating what would otherwise appear to be injustices and perhaps even multiplying them. This suggests another question: Given that injustice might be considered a form of cruelty, can something that is merciful also be unjust? While it is easy to see that mercy and justice might be independent, their antonyms 'cruelty' and 'injustice' are more easily aligned. So how could mercy displace justice entirely without creating the cruelty to which it is supposed to be the antidote?

THICK-THIN

Shklar herself treats cruelty and injustice as more or less coextensive and passes from cruelty to injustice without any indication that she perceives a discontinuity between the two. Indeed, she sees injustice as the more inclusive concept.[39] And since she gives no thought to mercy, she assumes that cruelty will be remedied by justice. However, this is unpersuasive. Cruelty and the potential for cruelty will be found in many circumstances where the idea of justice is simply inapplicable. Justice will not be of any help. Even in the appropriate circumstances, it is not clear that justice is the remedy that cruelty demands. The experience of cruelty is located (primarily but not exclusively) in the body, whereas justice is to be found in the relations between people and things. Though prisoners may be seeking justice, under torture they beg for mercy, not for a just measure of pain.

All of which points to the possibility not only that cruelty and injustice are independent, but also that they may not be concepts of exactly the same type. However, at one level, there does seem to be something shared. Philippa Foot argues that both are 'conceptually verdictive' in that they entail a final 'should' or 'should not': 'If and when it is unjust or cruel to withhold from someone something that one owes that person, then one necessarily acts badly in doing so'.[40] This is one reason Shklar prioritises both concepts. But are they, in fact, equally verdictive? It is not 'the injustice of cruelty' that accounts for our outrage, but the cruelty of cruelty, whereas the cruelty of injustice may weigh more heavily than the injustice itself.

And are they concepts of the same kind? One conceptual distinction that helps to clarify the differences is that between 'thick' and 'thin' ethical concepts. A 'thin' ethical concept tells us whether something is 'right' or 'wrong', 'good' or 'bad', without telling us very much else.[41] Indeed, those words themselves are standard examples of 'thin' concepts; they constitute guides to action (you ought to do what is right and not what is wrong) but do not in themselves suggest what sort of action that would entail. In contrast, thick ethical concepts are, as Williams puts it, 'world guided', in that 'the way these notions are applied is determined by what the world is like', and at the same time action-guiding in that their application 'usually involves a certain valuation of the situation, of persons or actions'.[42] Rather than being easily separable into a description and an ought, a thick ethical concept entangles the two in such a way that it is difficult to separate them.

Cruelty is perhaps the most often cited example of such a thick concept. As Hilary Putnam argues, 'cruel' functions both as a descriptive term ('the cruelties of fate', etc.) and as a normative one, and yet it seems impossible to disentangle the two: 'I cannot simply say, "He is a very cruel person and a good man", and be understood'.[43] By this measure 'cruel' is not just a verdictive concept but a thick one too. And that is surely its claim to priority—we know both that it is wrong and what sort of thing it is. But by these same criteria, injustice appears, if not thin, then at the very least thinner than 'cruel', in that although it usually has a similar normative value (there are exceptions: 'he is very unjust but he's a good man' could apply to someone who bestowed benefits capriciously), it is of less descriptive value, in that (without a specific context) it is almost impossible to know what will count as an injustice any more than it is possible to know what will count as a 'wrong move'. If cruelty is a thicker concept than injustice, then the prospect of multiplying injustices through the exercise of mercy may be less alarming than it sounds. Eliminating cruelty will bring an indubitable and tangible benefit, without our necessarily being able to determine whether the consequences are unjust or not.

On this basis, it is reasonable to suppose that mercy is thicker than justice as well. And though mercy is rarely discussed in this context, it is difficult to imagine what would serve as a thin account of mercy. All those things that are sometimes considered its defects as an evaluative term (e.g., its very particularity) keep it thick. Mercy involves a comparative judgement about particular circumstances, and though the context may change, those circumstances always have the same features. Despite the differing levels of specificity, there is not much difference between, say, 'mercy in warfare', 'discretionary mercy', and 'mercy', and there won't be much question as to whether something that counts as 'mercy in warfare' is indeed 'merciful' tout court. Whereas a purely evaluative concept can be understood independently of its object and tells us nothing about it, mercy not only tells us a great deal about the type of situation in which it is applicable, but has a descriptive element that is incapable of separate instantiation.

Justice too is sometimes held to be thick, and Williams claims that considerations of justice may be 'a central element of ethical thought that transcends the relativism of distance'.[44] But, as Scheffler points out, people who have the concept of justice will disagree about its application even in central cases, and to the extent that they do, it suggests that the concept of justice is not 'world-guided' at all.[45] As the terms of reference for justice fall away it becomes notably thinner. For example, 'just in Roman law' is thicker than 'distributively just', which in turn is thicker than 'just', and 'fair in cricket' is thicker than 'fair play', which in turn is thicker than 'fair'. In these cases, the descriptive element progressively diminishes and the evaluative takes over, with the result that there is almost no way of telling whether what is 'just in Roman law' or 'fair in cricket' will count as just or fair in an unqualified sense. The correct application of the term is world-guided in the first cases, but so exclusively action-guiding at the end, that the world seems to have slipped away.

The thick-thin distinction provides a useful way of articulating the relationship between justice and mercy in historical terms as well. If mercy is thicker than justice, this positions it somewhat differently within the genealogy of morals. According to Williams, modern ethical theory regards as basic 'very general or abstract ethical concepts—what may be called "thin" ethical concepts—and uses them to explain or, more significantly, to replace "thick" concepts with a relatively high descriptive content'.[46] In this context, the displacement of mercy by justice can be linked to the wider phenomenon already identified by Nietzsche, in which ethical codes embedded in existing forms of life were superseded by moralities built on supposedly rational foundations. Outside the original social context, however, Nietzsche maintains that 'talk of right and wrong ... is senseless'.[47] And Williams agrees, arguing that in practice thin concepts are 'too abstract and theoretical to provide any substance' for either private morality or public justification. The very idea that rationality requires ethical thought to be systematized on the basis of thin ethical concepts is mistaken; rather than 'trying to eliminate or reduce all "thick" concepts in the name of rationality, we should try to hold on to as many as we can'.[48]

It is within this context that arguments about justice that seem to incline towards mercy need to be viewed. Let's consider this with regard to two cases discussed earlier: Sen and Nussbaum. Sen's criticism of Rawls's ideal conception of justice is in large measure a critique of its thinness. The difficulty of using ideal justice to make comparative judgements about particular outcomes is characteristic of a thin concept whose criteria of application are unclear or indeterminate. In contrast, as Putnam noted, 'just about every one of the terms that Sen and his colleagues and followers use when they talk about capabilities ... is an entangled term'.[49] The move from ideal justice to the perspective of Smith's impartial spectator also counts as a move from thin to thick. The sympathy required for impartial spectatorship involves thickening as the spectator tries 'to put himself in the situation of the other, and to bring home to himself every little circumstance of distress which can possibly occur to the sufferer'.[50] Impartiality means involvement in the culturally and psychologically specific particulars of a given situation so that the justice that emerges from it is thicker than that of ideal theory.

A similar move is implied by Nussbaum, who also invokes Smith's impartial spectator in her account of equity.[51] Recognition of the particular circumstances of a case, and seeing it in the round, translates a more abstract conception of justice into one that fits an individual case as snugly as a leaden rule bent around the shape of the column. That leaden rule, whose evaluative length is inseparable from its descriptive shape, is a model of how entanglement works. And it helps to account for Nussbaum's 'unexplained connection between appropriate situational judgement and mercy'. There would be no need for equity if justice were applied in conditions that perfectly reproduced the circumstances that gave rise to it. The fact that equity is called for at all presupposes that, to some degree, the circumstances in which it is to be applied are more like those of mercy than those of justice. And equity will modify justice to take on the character of those circumstances, simultaneously making justice thicker and more merciful.

In the arguments above, thin concepts are either thickened or replaced by thicker ones. A comparable transition takes place in Williams's account of the Basic Legitimation Demand (BLD). Williams rejects political morality which claims 'the priority of the moral over the political'—i.e., application of thin abstract concepts which supposedly tell us what to do.[52] An answer to the first political question has to be one that is locally acceptable; it has to make sense 'in the light of historical circumstances'. 'Making sense' is, as Williams points out, 'itself an evaluative concept ... not simply "factual" or "descriptive"'.[53] It is, in other words, itself thick, and Williams supposes it will take a variety of thick local forms. What Sen's impartial spectator, Nussbaum's equity, and Williams's BLD have in common is that all are forms of thickening. What they do not do is go beyond that to challenge the originary exclusion on which post-Enlightenment accounts of justice are based—the exclusion of mercy.

Mercy disappeared from political discourse as part of the attempt to replace the thick concepts of traditional morality, based on countervailing passions, with thin ones deducible from rational self-interest. But the very scepticism that thinned ethical concepts in the first place eventually points us back towards thick concepts as the only possible form in which they will have traction in everyday life. As Montaigne and Nietzsche both emphasise, scepticism leaves us with more certainty about the needs and frailties of the body than about the truths discovered by reason. We find ourselves unable to determine what is for the best, but still desperate to avoid the worst. In this context, the underlying argument against the priority of justice is the same as that for putting cruelty first: in a disenchanted world we do not know enough and cannot endure enough to do otherwise. Mercy is the thick residue of our attempts at ethical ratiocination.

However, this does not mean that thick concepts are, of their very nature, more likely to be merciful in their application than thin ones. That is not the case. Nietzsche's thick conception of the good as an aristocratic virtue gives a license to cruelty that thinner conceptions of the good customarily do not.[54] But there is a connection. Like a leaden rule, a thick concept is shaped by the facts of the world in a way that a thin concept never is. Political realism embodies a preference for thick concepts over thin ones precisely because it wants to work with concepts that have an application in the real world rather than in an ideal one. As a result, the concepts of realism are going to have a different sort of shape to those of political morality, a shape that bears the imprint of the circumstances in which politics is called for: the dominance of the powerful and the vulnerability of the weak. That should not come as a surprise—realism in politics is famously about power rather than anything else. However, a thick concept will, insofar as it is evaluative, not just reflect but also imply some judgement regarding that asymmetry. In every case, therefore, a thick concept applicable to the circumstances of mercy will either affirm or seek to mitigate the effects of power.

Thus, the thick concepts of Nietzsche's revaluation of morality all either affirm or enhance underlying asymmetries of power. In contrast, the approaches cited above (mercy, equity, impartial spectatorship, making sense) appear to have the opposite effect. This is not wholly fortuitous. The argument of this chapter suggests that a thick concept applicable to the circumstances of mercy will have either a power-affirming or a power-denying effect. Why, then, do all these examples incline one way? Because, unlike Nietzsche's, they work from the premise that peace is preferable to war. If human association is to be more than a war of all against all, something other than power is required, and whatever it is must seek to mitigate or redress the effect of underlying differentials in power. Any realism, insofar as it is a *political* realism, will incline to mercy. But mercy, once permitted, has no clear limit. That is why Nietzsche prefers war.

4

If mercy is sufficient for politics, and mercy is sufficient for sociability, it might be supposed that mercy would be sufficient for the state. But that is not necessarily the case, which means that mercy requires us to consider the potential of politics without the state. That sounds daunting, because we often suppose that the state is a necessary condition of peace, and that politics without the state is war. We should not be too worried, however, for the state in the modern sense did not always exist. As Quentin Skinner points out, until the sixteenth century the Latin *status*, and its vernacular equivalents, was predominantly used to refer to 'the state or standing of rulers themselves'. How to *mantenere lo stato* in the sense of the *stato del principe* is the focus of Machiavelli and other writers of mirrors for princes, but the implication is that the *stato del principe* is just the state of the prince having power over others (*imperio sopra li uomini*), and that that state exists only as long as that is the case. Machiavelli did not understand the state 'as an agent whose existence remains independent of those who exercise its authority at any given time'. The idea comes from later writers in the republican tradition, who start to differentiate between the status of the ruler and the state over which they rule. Even so, this does not express 'the modern understanding of the state as an authority distinct from rulers and ruled'. Republican writers only distinguish the state from the rulers, not from the ruled. It is Hobbes who first argues that 'the state is distinct from both'.[1]

Hobbes differentiates the state from the ruled by insisting that there is a distinction to be made between the multitude of individuals who inhabit a place, and 'the multitude ... united into a body politic'.[2] This involves a covenant in which each individual covenants with every other to give up their right of self-government in favour of a sovereign. This united body is the state distinct both from the multitude and the authorized sovereign to whom authority is given (whether monarchy, aristocracy, or democracy). The state is 'One Person, of whose Acts a great Multitude, by mutuall Covenants one with another, have made themselves every one the Author', while the sovereign is 'he that carryeth this Person ... and [is] said to have Soveraigne Power; and every one besides, his SUBJECT'.[3] The effect of this move is not only to differentiate the state from ruler and ruled, but to make it into the mechanism through which the ruled may be said to be ruling themselves. Hence, 'the nature of a commonwealth is that a multitude of citizens both exercises power and is subject to power, but in different senses', and in this regard a principality is no different to a republic.[4]

This argument not only puts to rest Machiavelli's idea that the state is just the state of having power over, but also undermines any notion that the balance between cruelty and mercy might be decisive for its continued success. If the people are the authors of the actions of the sovereign, then they cannot be said to be in the circumstances of mercy, for they are self-governing, and any harm done to them by the sovereign is in a sense authored by themselves. Hobbes's account of the state therefore seems to exclude mercy as effectively as the circumstances and principles of justice. However, a close reading suggests that it too relies on mercy, both in the circumstances of the contract and in Hobbes's far less well-known descriptions of the alternative routes to society.

According to Hobbes, the Leviathan represents the alternative to the war of all against all, and it is because everyone is at the mercy of everyone else that the state of nature demands some form of social compact in the first place: 'nature has made men so equall ... that the weakest has strength enough to kill the strongest'.[5] There are two ways this claim might be interpreted: (1) that everyone, at all times, has an equal power to harm, and is in a constant state of readiness for battle;

and (2) that there is a sequence of moments in each of which the power to harm is unequal, and some are ready for battle and others not. (For example: one person is a child when another an adult; one is asleep while another is awake, etc.) It does not follow from 'All are vulnerable at some time' that 'All are vulnerable at all times' or that 'All are equally vulnerable', let alone that 'All are equally vulnerable at all times'. So (2) is the only plausible interpretation. If everyone had equal power to harm at all times, each could frustrate the harmful actions of the other. Everyone is at the mercy of everyone else not because everyone is at the mercy of everyone else at all times, but rather because everyone is at the mercy of someone else at some time.

Given that the state of war embodies the circumstances of mercy, is there any prospect for departure from it that does not presuppose the exercise of mercy? According to Hobbes, the law of pardon or mercy (*misericordia* in *De Cive*) is nothing but the 'granting of peace' to someone who gives a guarantee or caution for the future.[6] This suggests that peace can be granted unilaterally by those with the power to do so, and it implies that in any one of those moments in which men are unequal, mercy might ensure peace between them. A time of peace would be a continuous succession of such moments. And this must, in fact, be the situation presupposed by Hobbes's account of the contract, because for a social contract to be possible those involved must already have been spared in the sense that they have not been killed. Hobbes argues that mercy, and the other laws of nature, are necessary for peace, but that they succeed the covenant because they are contrary to the natural passions and otherwise unenforceable. Yet even if this were true, the transition from the state of war to the covenant would have to be preceded by peace granted in this manner (with or without a caution), because otherwise the covenant could not be made. If everyone is at the mercy of someone else, they must already be in some way beneficiaries of mercy in order to contract with one another.

It is easier to see this if one considers the alternative hypothesis—namely, that people are so unequal that all are subject to the power of one person. In such circumstances, peace would depend on that person's mercy continuing from one moment to the next. Nevertheless, it would be a time of peace for as long as it lasted, so the same would be true if the time were composed of a multitude of such moments and granted by multiple agents. Hobbes actually goes further, and in *De Cive* makes clear that 'in the natural state of man sure and irresistible power gives the right of ruling and commanding those who cannot resist'. In these circumstances, power over (whether the result of infancy, weakness, or inability to resist) combined with mercy is sufficient for peace.[7]

In fact, as finally becomes clear in *Leviathan*, 'despotical dominion' acquired by conquest, or victory in war, is not just something that happens within the state of nature, but actually constitutes an alternative route to the civil state:

> The attaining to this Soveraigne Power is by two wayes. One, by Naturall force: as when a man maketh his children, to submit themselves, and their children, to his government, as being able to destroy them if they refuse; or by Warre subdueth his enemies to his will, giving them their lives on that condition. The other, is when men agree amongst themselves to submit to some Man, or Assembly of men, voluntarily, on confidence to be protected by him against all others. This latter may be called a Politicall Commonwealth, or Common-wealth by *Institution*; and the former, a Common-wealth by *Acquisition*.[8]

Unlike commonwealth by institution, commonwealth by acquisition is formed directly from within the circumstances of mercy, and by the exercise of mercy.

When Hobbes first explores this theme in the *Elements*, while acknowledging that 'Commonwealth' can function as the generic name for both, he makes a distinction between a 'body politic' that arises naturally 'from whence proceedeth dominion, paternal, and despotic', and one formed 'by mutual agreement among many', which is 'for the most part called a commonwealth in distinction from the former'.[9] In *De Cive*, he calls both a *civitas*, while distinguishing 'the natural commonwealth (*civitas naturalis*) which may also be called a commonwealth by acquisition since it is acquired by natural power and strength' and 'the commonwealth by design (*civitas institutiva*), the commonwealth which is initiated by an accord between a number of men, binding themselves to each other'.[10] But in *Leviathan*, he makes a determined effort to align the former with the latter, arguing that it 'differeth from Soveraignty by Institution onely in this, That men who choose their Soveraign do it for fear of one another, and not of him whom they Institute: But in this case, they subject themselves, to him they are afraid of'. Consequently 'the Rights and Consequences of both Paternall and Despoticall Dominion, are the very same with those of a Soveraign by Institution; and for the same reasons'.[11]

Hobbes claims that both are based on a binding covenant. However, this not only elides the distinction between a covenant based on mutual fear and one made by the vanquished 'to avoid the present stroke of death'; it also omits entirely the crucial original step in Hobbes's theory of the state: namely that it is a covenant that men make with one another that forms the state, and not a covenant with the sovereign, or the designation of a sovereign.[12] The Leviathan is one person, of whose acts the multitude have covenanted to make themselves the author, not the sovereign who 'carryeth this Person', and the relationship that constitutes the state is the binding contract the multitude make with each other and not the relation of sovereign and subject. Without this we just have dominion, Machiavelli's *imperio sopra li uomini*, and the concept of the state no longer refers to anything independent of the dyad of ruler and ruled.

This conclusion has far-reaching implications. If Hobbes accepts that pardon granted by one man is enough for a *civitas*, it follows that overlapping pardons granted by many individuals would also be sufficient, and that a dispersed dominion would be as effective a way to bring about peace as one where a single despot had power over everyone else. Hobbes insists that commonwealth by acquisition is grounded not in mercy alone but in binding promises—promises made at the point of the sword, or by infants to their fathers, or by some sign from the enfeebled. This stipulation has never seemed particularly persuasive to anyone who assumes that lasting agreements can only be made on the basis of free and informed consent. And Hobbes's claim that a peace granted without caution would only be granted on the basis of fear of the vanquished is inapplicable to many of these cases (e.g., fathers and their infants).[13] However, the primary question is not whether such guarantees are meaningful, but whether they are necessary for peace (as opposed to the Hobbesian commonwealth). And they are clearly not, for it is possible to have peace without a truce. Even Hobbes's definition of war in the *Elements* and *De Cive* allows for this: war is not battle only, but 'that time wherein the will and inclination of contending by force is sufficiently declared'. It is only in *Leviathan* that he adds 'all the time there is no assurance to the contrary'.[14] In the former case the default situation is peace, in the latter it is war. And if the latter account is wrong (as it surely is), then no caution is necessary.[15]

If the covenant presupposes that everyone making it has received sufficient mercy from someone (not everyone) else to be alive rather than dead, then the state of affairs presupposed by the covenant is nothing other than this dispersed form of dominion, in which case the covenant itself is not necessary for peace, for a form of peace without subjection to a sovereign already exists. In these circumstances, the covenant of all with all is at best a bonus, at worst superfluous.

COMPLEASANCE

Hobbes recognises that what he calls 'Peace without subjection'—peace without a 'common Power to keep them all in awe'—might be a route to sociability.[16] In his view, however, it is unsuited to humans and can be found only amongst social animals, and he never gives a systematic account of how this 'peace without subjection' comes about. But there are enough indications to show how it would work. In *Leviathan* he calls the process 'where mens wills are to be wrought to our purpose, [but] not by Force ... Compleasance'.[17] Hobbes makes compleasance into the fifth law of nature and describes it as the law 'that every man strive to accommodate himselfe to the rest'. However, the nomenclature is unstable, and this is the same law that he had designated 'Charity' in the *Elements*. There he makes clear that this is a countervailing passion ('seeing the causes of war and desolation proceed from those passions, by which we strive to accommodate ourselves ... it followeth that that passion by which we strive mutually to accommodate each other, must be the cause of peace') and that it incorporates mercy: 'In this precept of nature is included and comprehended also this, That a man forgive and pardon him that hath done him wrong, upon his repentance, and caution for the future'.[18]

The word 'compleasance' or 'complaisance' comes from French manuals for artistocratic behaviour, and, according to Hobbes, 'it signifieth as much as Courting, that is, a winning of favour by good offices'.[19] Joseph Addison hyperbolically identified 'complaisance' as what 'distinguishes a Society of civilized Persons from a Confusion of Savages', and though Hobbes does not go so far, in *Leviathan* he acknowledged that observers of the law of complaisance might be called 'sociable', rather like the animals that he later says 'live sociably one with another'.[20] Since for Hobbes the laws of nature are not operative in the state of nature, and applicable only after the covenant has been established, he does not allow that complaisance could ever be the origin of human society. But there is an inconsistency here. Although compleasance involves no 'common power', if it encompasses pardon, which in despotical dominion suffices for the transition to society, it too should be able to foster sociability without a covenant, albeit in a dispersed or localised form.

Hobbes likens compleasance to 'stones brought together for building of an Aedifice'.[21] Someone who takes more from others than he needs for himself is like a hard and irregular stone that requires more space than it can fill and is unusable, and compleasance is the process of adjustment by which people fit in with each other, smoothing the rough edges so that they can be together. As Hobbes makes clear, there is no requirement that everyone be involved for the structure to take shape, or for all the stones to fit together in order for any of them to fit together. All that is needed is for one stone to fit with another, and a stone that does not fit can just be left to one side. This makes the edifice that takes shape into something closer to Hume's wall of benevolence than to his vault of justice, and it shows just how close compleasance is to Hume's 'gentle usage'. Indeed, in the eighteenth century they were virtually synonymous, and Hume himself used the term 'complaisance' to refer to men's gentle treatment of women.[22]

According to Hobbes, compleasance is exemplified by not striving 'to retain those things which to himself are superfluous, and to others necessary'.[23] This assumes a substantial difference in economic power: one party has a superfluity of goods, while the other lacks even the necessities. No examples are offered, but the ancient pirates Hobbes mentions elsewhere who lived by plunder, but spared life, plough oxen, and agricultural equipment, might be seen to be acting exactly in accordance with this principle even though they were restrained by no laws, including those of nature, and acted as they did only because they did not want a reputation for cruelty.[24] This is an extreme example, but in contrast to the unrestrained plunder of the New World by European colonists to which Hume refers, Hobbes's pirates have good manners. Without contracts or conventions, that is all you have, and maybe all you need.

But where does it get you? What sort of sociability does complaisance afford? Making two uneven stones fit together is much more like 'converging on a passing theory' than anything else, because it does not specify that all stones should fit together, or the way that they should fit together, or even that two similar stones should fit together in the same way the next time. The process is thus more akin to the 'rational accommodation' required for 'radical sociability' than a covenant or convention, but the result is a form of sociability nevertheless. And if so, it suggests that, even on Hobbes's terms, we can make no absolute distinction between peace achieved though despotical dominion and through complaisance. In both cases, all that is required is restraint in the exercise of power. And although the former assumes force (e.g., victory in war) while the latter is achieved without it, the difference is a matter of degree. Sometimes, as in the case of parents and children, it may be difficult to distinguish between the two.

STATELESS STATES

The Hobbesian state is a person distinct from both rulers and ruled. Mercy is necessary for it, but not sufficient. However, mercy is sufficient for those other forms of association which Hobbes calls 'despotical dominion' and 'peace without subjection'. So even on Hobbes's account it looks as though, thanks to mercy, it might be possible to have peace without the state. This suggests that the first 'Hobbesian' question might be susceptible to a different answer to the one Williams offers. Williams supposes it to be 'a necessary condition of legitimacy that the state solve the first question'.[25] But is it necessary for *the state* to solve the question, or is it necessary only that the question be solved?

If all that is needed for peace is that domination be acceptable rather than legitimate, and acceptability is of its very nature a graduated concept, the difference between peace and war is one of degree. And if society itself does not necessarily involve a monopoly of power, but may be dispersed and fragmentary, it follows that, far from having a stark choice between the war of all against all and a legitimate state, there is scope for varying forms and degrees of both power over and acceptance. On this account, there is no absolute distinction between war and peace, and no clear boundary between peace without subjection and peace with subjection. Mercy is required in each case, and insofar as all are forms of peace rather than war, they are examples of political life. In practice, however, our experience may involve a confusing combination of all of these forms, their hybrids and overlaps, interspersed with attempts to sustain microspheres of justice, and, perhaps more often than we acknowledge, periods that are closer to war.

Where does this leave the idea of the state? It certainly does not seem to require the Hobbesian idea of the covenant of all with all, or even a covenant between the victor and the vanquished, so why do we need to talk about the state at all? The current fiction of a world divided into discrete states whose legitimacy is mutually recognized barely accounts for contemporary reality, let alone the historical experience of power. Skinner describes the concept of the state emerging through differentiation from both rulers and ruled. But is the state really something distinct from the rulers and the ruled? There are two ways this question might be posed: whether there is a distinct referent as Hobbes claims, and whether the state is distinct from the relation of ruling and being ruled. The former is not the case without the covenant, so in that sense the state does not exist; but what about the latter? In what sense, if any, might the state be said to exist as a result of mercy shown in 'despotical dominion' or 'peace without subjection'?

Derek Parfit's analogy between personhood and the personhood of the state may suggest a model. For example, it might be possible to believe *both* that a state involves the existence of people living together in certain ways in a geographical area *and* that a state is an entity distinct from its people and its area, rather as one might believe *both* that 'a person's existence just consists in the existence of a brain and body', *and* that 'a person is an entity that is *distinct* from a brain and body'. This may sound like having your cake and eating it, but it incorporates the reductionist view that 'we could give a complete description of reality without claiming that states or persons exist' while acknowledging that persons and states exist as something distinct from these things because we can successfully refer to them in a way that we cannot refer to nonexistent persons and things. (For example, we can refer to the Italian state in a way that we cannot refer to the state of Ruritania.)[26]

But if we accept the reductionist view of the state, what are we reducing it to? What is the state of affairs that we refer to when we refer to the state? Weber's definition of the state as 'a human community that (successfully) claims the monopoly of the legitimate use of physical force within a given territory' suggests that only monopoly and full acceptance will do.[27] (And this is true of the Hobbesian state as well.) But there is also a temporal dimension. As Williams emphasizes, 'A solution to the first political question is required *all the time*'.[28] How is all-the-timeness delivered? It could theoretically be delivered by individual acts of mercy, each distinct in their agency and motivation, aligned in such a way as to be seamless. But there are, in practice, breakdowns and discontinuities in any wall of mercy, though these may be minimised where there is continuity of agency—i.e., where mercy is granted repeatedly by the same agent.

So, although there is no fundamental difference between the mercy needed for mere sociability and that required for politics, what we call a state involves a sustained monopoly of power mercifully exercised for a long period of time in a particular location. But it is nothing more than that: just a continuous sequence of voluntary actions and inactions by those with, at that moment, power over. Yet if the state consists in the merciful exercise of the power of life and death over time, in what sense is it distinct from those people and that action? Only in the same sense that other objects are distinct from what John Searle calls 'the continuous possibility of the activity'.[29] In other words, we do not necessarily need a theory of the state that is different to the theory that we need to explain the emergence of any other institutional facts. It is just another agentive function on which a status function has been imposed. Thus, in the transition from the *stato del principe* to the state, the status function of the state is imposed on the princely activity of exercising power over. This is a linguistic move, but not necessarily a performative one (it might be argued that Hobbes confuses these two things): not a change in the brute facts, but a change in the way they are described.

There are two implications of this, which, when applied to political theory, are potentially as surprising as Parfit's claims about personal identity. The first is that the facts about a state can be described without either presupposing the identity of the state, or explicitly claiming that the events in this history are those of the state, or even explicitly claiming that the state exists—in other words, that the history of the state could, without loss, be narrated in an *anarchic* way.[30] The second is that the very existence of a state might be seen as indeterminate. In other words, the facts could be exhaustively described, while allowing for uncertainty about whether this was or was not a state, or the same state that had existed previously.[31] The idea of the state might therefore be 'distinct from' the relationship of rulers and the ruled, yet still able to be described without loss in terms of that relationship, and also not so distinct that it was possible (or perhaps interesting) to determine whether its identity at t^1 was the same as that at t^2.

CONSEQUENCES OF THE ABOVE

The modern theory of the state, like the modern theory of justice, develops alongside, and to some degree depends on, the repudiation of mercy. Hobbes was writing at a time when monarchy was still legitimating its authority through pardons, and, in 1662, afraid of being prosecuted for heresy, he himself claimed the protection of Charles II's 'gracious general pardon'.[32] Nevertheless, he seeks to exclude mercy from his account of state formation, for the perspective of mercy is liable to destabilise it and take us back to earlier ad hoc conceptions of statehood. Hobbes's Leviathan is a 'mortal god' in the tradition of monotheism who embodies the idea that the state is singular, necessary, eternal, and irresistible. That is why it seems to need a social ontology all its own. In contrast, the power relations within which mercy is exercised are usually multiple, contingent, discontinuous, and reversible. The power over that mercy makes acceptable has at least four features that the Hobbesian theory of state would preclude: it is not unique, it depends on luck, and the relationships within it are nonreciprocal and inherently unstable.

States may claim a monopoly of force, but our political lives are far more complex than any theory of state will allow. The reality is usually that we are the subjects of many masters. Even when continuous, mercy is not necessarily exclusive to one agent, because being at the mercy of is not an exclusive relationship; just as someone can have multiple subjects, they may have multiple masters (who may, in turn, be nested in complex power relationships of their own). For example, let's suppose that I run a small business. Every Tuesday, someone comes round and says, 'Your shop could easily burn down, but if you pay me $5 I'll make sure it will not'. On Wednesday, someone else comes round and says the same thing. I am a cautious person and pay both individuals. This situation is, of course, not just theoretically possible: forms of it exist when people have to deal with rival crime syndicates, or a government and a gang, or with the competing claims of different systems of thought—those of missionaries and traditional specialists, or alternative systems of medicine. Hedging your bets in this way is quite common, and not only in revolutionary situations where multiple would-be sovereigns are in competition for a monopoly position.[33] During the Cold War most people, nations, and international organisations were at the mercy of the two nuclear superpowers and acted accordingly. Both superpowers had found an 'acceptable' solution to the problem of order at a global level, not just in their respective spheres of influence, but as a duopoly.

As this example reminds us, although post-Hobbesian theories of the state offer the illusion that we are masters of our own destiny, we are not. Our very survival depends upon the forbearance of others over whom we have no control. This should not surprise us; if politics is a function of the continued merciful exercise of power, then it follows that politics is a matter of luck.[34] There are several senses in which this might be true, and all have disquieting implications. First, having power over is itself largely a matter of luck, dependent on a variety of contingencies. It is a function of geography, historical circumstances, all the decisions of previous generations, a lottery of genetic factors, and so on. This is an empirical claim, and it is not particularly controversial where relative power is concerned. But it does imply that having power over does not necessarily raise the question, before its exercise, of whether it is acceptable or not. And if the ability to exercise mercy is only available to those with power over, and having power over is a matter of luck, then the political virtue of mercy is something only the lucky can ever possess. This is a controversial claim in modern times, because it goes against the ideals of democratic citizenship. But if the state is just a power relation, there is no clear way of determining who is or is not a citizen anyway. And given that few have the power to exercise fully the citizenship rights they notionally possess, most may be more accurately described as subjects in any case.

Furthermore—and this is where the idea of political luck intersects with that of moral luck—luck-dependent outcomes (e.g., the variable capacity of subjects to rebel) will also determine whether mercy is exercised acceptably. Indeed, this is clear enough in political (un-like moral) contexts, where success or failure more clearly determines retrospective judgements.[35] To be politically successful is to be powerful, merciful, and lucky (the last inseparable from the former). This is perhaps the only retrospective positive political judge-ment a historian can make, but it excludes any idea of legitimacy. The circumstantial luck that puts you in a position to exercise mercy undermines the idea that there is legitimacy before the exercise of mercy. But if resultant luck is as important as circumstantial luck, then the successful exercise of mercy does not legiti-mize circumstantial power either. And if receiving mercy is just as much a matter of luck as the ability to bestow it successfully, this precludes any argument to the effect that mercy is a human right, because you cannot have a right to something that you can only receive as a matter of luck. So, in one go, mercy threat-ens legitimacy, citizenship, and human rights.[36]

And yet the most surprising, and perhaps alarm-ing, implication of this argument is to be found else-where. The asymmetry in power relations presupposed by mercy excludes the possibility of reciprocity in the sense that no one who receives mercy is simultaneously able to give mercy in return. For politics to be possi-ble, the powerful must be merciful. Insofar as they are powerless, the weak are not in a position to exercise mercy themselves. Of course, almost no one is entirely powerless, or powerless all of the time, but, relative to those who have power over them, the vulnerable are not in a position to harm. So, no mercy can be expected from the weak, because they are by definition never in a position to offer it. They are merciless in the sense that they cannot exercise mercy.

It might be argued that there are ways in which reciprocity might work even in situations of asymmetry.[37] Power relations are positions, not identities, so, were they to be reversed, politics would require mercy from those who were formerly weak but are now powerful. If it were required *because* it had been shown by those who were now its recipients, then that would be reciprocity. Alternatively (or perhaps additionally) if someone receives mercy from another, they can reciprocate not by returning the favour to the one who bestowed it, but rather by offering mercy to someone else. Edmund Burke argued that society 'is a partnership not only between those who are living, but between those who are living, those who are dead and those who are to be born'.[38] And it is possible to argue for indirect reciprocity on the basis that having received an inheritance from their ancestors each generation has an obligation to pass it on to their descendants rather than appropriate it for themselves.

However, luck undermines the argument for both these forms of reciprocity. If it is the result of luck, the fact that you have received mercy doesn't obviously create an obligation that you did not have before. If I win the lottery, I am not obliged to give a fortune back to the lottery company at a later date, or to pass on the money to an undeserving stranger.[39] There may be good reasons to be merciful in your turn, but these are moral arguments (e.g., it is good to help the needy) rather than political ones internal to the relationship produced by mercy. You only have reciprocal obligations if you are already in a reciprocal relationship. Reciprocity itself requires not luck but luck egalitarianism, because arbitrary inequalities must be reduced for reciprocity to be maintained.[40] And if luck is necessary for mercy, then you cannot automatically be blamed for being unmerciful, because you may just lack the lucky breaks that would allow you to be so. There is a marked contrast with justice here. Justice not only presupposes reciprocity but entails it: everyone behaves justly with respect to everyone else; the idea that some might be expected to act justly, and others not, would be incompatible with the principle of justice itself.

Nonreciprocity in the case of mercy means both a lack of obligation to be merciful to those who have shown you mercy, and a lack of obligation to be merciful to anyone else as a result of having received mercy. The merciless weak are therefore in a similar position to that Hobbes attributes to the defeated person who has made no covenant with the victor but 'is kept in prison, or bonds, till the owner of him that took him, or bought him of one that did, shall consider what to do with him'. According to Hobbes, such persons 'have no obligation at all; but may break their bonds, or the prison; and kill, or carry away captive their master, justly'.[41] Hobbes is describing a state of war, so how much restraint is needed from the powerless for politics to be possible? In the political state, the power of life and death must be exercised mercifully by all, and other powers must be exercised sufficiently mercifully by the powerful for the powerless not to choose war. However, the powerless are under no corresponding obligation to do less harm than they might, and certainly not less than it is in their interests to do. If, as Hobbes says, they have no 'obligation at all', they may freely 'break their bonds, or the prison', although they cannot 'kill, or carry away captive their master' without having power over, in which case the roles are reversed, and it is they and not their former masters who have the opportunity to avoid war through the merciful exercise of power. For the first political question to be satisfied, the weak cannot be at war with the strong any more than the strong can be making war on the weak. But because there is no symmetry or reciprocity between them, for politics to be possible mercy is required from the powerful but not from the weak. All that is required from them is a merciless peace.

OVERPOWERING

But what would a merciless peace be like? Is it not a contradiction in terms? A merciless peace does not imply the permanent acceptance of existing power relations, only a contingent acceptance of the exercise of

that power combined with a potentially relentless resistance to it. As James C. Scott has argued, this is the
norm rather than the exception: 'Most of the political
life of subordinate groups is to be found neither in the
overt collective defiance of powerholders nor in complete hegemonic compliance, but in the vast territory
between these two polar opposites'.[42] Any degree of
compliance is heavily dependent on the mercy of the
powerful, and is easily lost through some act of cruelty, but everyday resistance can continue alongside it,
as an attritional strategy that may eventually succeed in
modifying or even overturning the power imbalance
it is designed to resist.[43]

But can the weak really overpower the strong if
they do not have power already and do not go to war?
Can overpowering take place *within* politics? Even in
Hume's thought experiment, where the species of creatures intermingled with men is said to be 'incapable
of all resistance', he suggests that the everyday resistance of women (Hume characterises it as their 'in-
sinuation, address, and charms') might break the male
stranglehold on power and allow them to share 'all the
rights and privileges of society'.[44] If the mercy of the
powerful creates no reciprocal obligation for the powerless, then the scope of what we might think of as
politics as opposed to war is both contracted and expanded. In war the strong defeat the weak. But if politics is mercy, then it is necessarily the case that the
strong do the weak less harm than they would if they

were at war. Furthermore, given that being vulnerable is itself a form of harm, mercy excludes enhancing power over. So when you already have power over you cannot gain more *political* power unmercifully. That is tyranny, and tyrants are engaged not in politics but in internalized warfare with their own people. You cannot reduce a section of your own population from citizenship to slavery, let alone transform a weak neighbouring ally into a province, without it being an act of war.

The asymmetry between those who have power over and those who are vulnerable to them produces a corresponding asymmetry in the range of actions that might be considered politics rather than war. Whereas increasing harm to the vulnerable is war, the same action against those with power over may still be politics. Making the vulnerable more vulnerable may be an act of cruelty, but making the powerful more vulnerable is not (at least until such point as you might be said to have power over), because not everything that is to someone's disadvantage counts as harm; in particular, losing some or all of your power over another person does not necessarily count as a harm to you.

This has significant consequences. If having power over is itself harmful, any voluntary reduction in power over will be an act of mercy. And if mercy reduces harm, then acts of mercy will reduce power over, if only by strengthening the relative position of the weak. (Even someone on death row may be marginally empowered by receiving a stay of execution.) Since mercy has no limit, there is no specified end to this process, which means that (other things being equal) the indefinite continuation of politics will inevitably reduce differentials in power. If at the same time the powerless act in their own interest against the interests of the powerful (as they are entirely free to do), then they are likely to become more powerful, and so ultimately overpower the powerful and become more powerful themselves. From this it follows that the continuation of politics uninterrupted by war will ultimately result in the overturning of power relations. Any politics based on mercy retains the instability of war but changes the likely outcome. In politics uninterrupted by war, the weak defeat the strong. Politics does not specify who should rule, but it has a counterhegemonic bias. Far from being incompatible with it, overpowering *is* politics, and anything else is war.

This conclusion is perhaps surprising, given the starting point of the discussion. Following Hobbes, Williams argues that politics is characterized by peace as opposed to war, and that there can be no peace unless those who are subject to power agree to stop fighting against their subjection. He suggests that this acceptance is given when the rule of the powerful is legitimated to the satisfaction of the ruled (in terms that make sense within the context of a particular time and place). If nothing changes, there is no reason why such legitimacy should not be acceptable in perpetuity. However, if acceptance is the result of mercy rather than legitimation, then the merciless weak will (if they act consistently in their own interests, but without recourse to war) eventually find that they have overturned the imbalance of power that existed at the outset. On this account, politics (as opposed to war) can never maintain the status quo.

Does that mean that conquest is possible within politics as well? No; it is by definition impossible to take power within politics unless the other party previously had power over you, because otherwise there is no existing political relationship to modify. If you have no previous contact with a neighbour and seek to overpower them, then that is an act of war rather than peace. But if your neighbour had power over you, and you overpowered them, then that is just overpowering within an existing political relationship and is not necessarily an act of conquest. Anyone whose power is political is liable to lose it within politics (through being merciful to the merciless). The idea that those in power may, within the scope of politics, be overpowered by those who are not is less radical than it sounds, and almost all modern political theories make some allowance for the possibility. Democratic elections are one mechanism for it, though how successful they are at bringing it about is debatable. But mercy is much more positive about overpowering than any theory of justice, and a politics grounded in it is always potentially revolutionary. Without either a theory of the state or a theory of justice to secure their position, those with power cannot complain if they are over-powered by those over whom that power is exercised. It is just political luck, Machiavelli's *fortuna*.

SPONGIFORM STATES

This argument has implications not only for the balance of power within what is thought of as the state, but also for that between the state and those within its wider sphere of influence. Conceived in terms of power, the boundaries of the state are indeterminate, and every state is what Williams once called 'a spongiform state' in that the scope of its politics is not coterminous with the national borders but extends to include all those who are vulnerable to it.[45] This will obviously be true of any nation that is more powerful than its neighbours; it will also apply if there are more distant communities who are in a state of economic dependency by virtue of trade, or who are liable to suffer the environmental effects of its pollution or whatever. The idea of the state serves to make invulnerable the position of those who have power over others outside of it. For Hobbes and later state theorists, it is the duty of the commonwealth 'to preserve people in peace at home and defend them against foreign invasion'.[46] But if the state is just the state of having power over, the absence of reciprocal obligations means that, unless or until the roles are reversed, those noncitizens over whom the state has power may, within the scope of politics, overpower the state powers that have power over them. For example, the colonized, peoples under armies of occupation, citizens of neighbouring countries within the sphere of influence, or even those subject to asymmetrical trading relationships might take over a whole or part of a nation-state.

What this means in practice is that the powerless may invade the nation-state that has power over them. That might seem shocking, but it falls short of military invasion, which would be war and not peace, while leaving open the possibility of things such as dramatic cross-border population movement and decisive transnational political action. Political theory, which supposedly constitutes some sort of guide to the way politics is or ought to be conducted, provides little account of such invasions, notwithstanding the fact that many existing nations are shaped by them. In just the same way that a metropolis that dominates the surrounding countryside may, within the scope of what we normally understand to be politics, be transformed by inward migration, with the result that the newcomers eventually take power from those who had it previously, so too the nation-state whose power extends beyond its borders may be transformed from without.

That is far from being the end of it. There is another assumption built into the account of the state which mercy also dissolves—the assumption that the only form of politics is within the human species. It is clear that animals and other natural species are at the mercy of the human one, and this is one area in which cruelty rather than justice or contract is already acknowledged to be a central issue. However, the situation is transformed when other species are not assumed to be outside the sphere of politics. Rather than being excluded from the benefits of a citizenship defined and defended by speciesist laws, other species are as much the potential subjects of politics as are humans. Sociability, and, at the very least, peaceful coexistence between humans and other species is obviously a possibility. And, being within the circumstances of mercy, it is clear that mercy is necessary to bring that about. The other side of this is that nonhuman species may subject the human one to a merciless resistance without it constituting war. Invasive species provide a model, and if enough species were invasive, the human one might struggle to retain its power.

The third state that is customarily taken as constituting a political boundary is the present. Temporal relationships provide an excellent example of the circumstances of mercy in that they constitute a chain of (nonreciprocal and) asymmetrical relationships. The asymmetry of the relation is relatively clear: those who had agency in the past have more power over people in the present than vice versa, and they in turn have more power over future generations than future generations do over them (unless they overlap). Modern politics was born of the belief that the past should not have undue power over the present, and that we must contend 'for the rights of the living'.[47] And (as we have seen) the presupposition of simultaneity is embedded in theories of the contract and of justice. Yet that assumes that each new generation has an equal capacity to make things over again from the beginning rather than being burdened with an unwanted legacy not of their choosing. If 'the aim of each generation' is, as Alexander Herzen claimed, 'itself', then for future generations the absolute rights of the living may turn out to be a form of tyranny.[48]

If mercy is the cure for tyranny in the present, it would seem that it should also be able to perform the same function for future generations. But this is not straightforward. As in other cases, the argument for mercy is not primarily moral (i.e., that mercy is morally preferable to its alternatives, though such a claim might of course be made) but rather political: the idea that mercy creates peace and facilitates sociability instead of war by making life more acceptable for the powerless. But there are circumstances in which the divide between the powerful and the powerless is so absolute that the idea of acceptability seems inapplicable, because its alternative—war—would be nonsensical, given that there is no causal mechanism through which any form of resistance, however futile or suicidal, might be pursued. This is certainly true of future generations (and of some, but not all, nonhuman species). The future victims of the present are trapped by time, unable to defend themselves retroactively or even to run further into the future. Meanwhile, the tyranny of the present has no negative consequences for the tyrants. Given that future generations cannot disturb our tranquillity, however merciless they may be, there would appear to be no argument in favour of peace. Mercy might still curb our tyranny, but the result would not make the difference between peace and war, and so it would not be politics (it would be warfare tempered with mercy).

However, although the unborn cannot make political choices now, their interests could be registered through a form of what Edmund Burke called 'virtual representation'. In this 'there is a communion of interests, and a sympathy in feelings and desires between those who act in the name of any description of people, and the people in whose name they act, though the trustees are not actually chosen by them'.[49] The current generation of human beings may of necessity furnish the representatives, but it does not follow that it is in its entirety an appropriate virtual representative of other generations, for it is collectively liable to prefer its own interests to theirs. Other generations will be more adequately represented by that minority best equipped to act for them.

Burke's idea has until recently received little theoretical attention, but virtual representation is an established part of governance, both in the form of elected representatives who represent the interests of particular groups outside their constituency (sometimes called 'surrogate representatives') and NGOs who take it upon themselves to represent the interests of groups (e.g., children, animals, the impoverished in developing countries) who are the beneficiaries of their campaigns but have played no part in their formation and may, indeed, sometimes be completely unaware of their activities. That being the case, it is less of a stretch than might be imagined to claim that future people, or other species, or indeed the future members of other species, might also have virtual representatives on the basis that they too have objective interests that can successfully be represented by others in the absence of both authorization and accountability.[50]

Yet if that is the case, why should not the dead, or the hypothetical inhabitants of as yet undiscovered planets, also have virtual representation? The difference is that they are not in the circumstances of mercy. They are invulnerable, and the invulnerable are in no need of politics because they have nothing to fear.[51] Power and vulnerability are the precondition of politics, and the inhabitants of the earth have at present no power over the past, nor other planets. Power over is a relationship that creates the possibility for tyranny and cruelty, and it is in the objective interests of the powerless to avoid or mitigate such consequences. A virtual representative is someone who acts to mitigate the cruelty of the powerful towards those they represent. They are virtual representatives by that fact alone (because not being killed or treated cruelly is in everyone's interests), and they are virtual representatives because of the positions they take, not because they are designated, or because of who they are. The argument in favour of virtual representation comes directly from putting cruelty first in the circumstances of mercy.

Like a Leninist vanguard (in which, as Georg Lukács puts it, the party represents 'the future of mankind'), the virtual representatives of future generations will press their claims against those of the living.[52] The powerful must, in general, be merciful if there is to be politics rather than war; otherwise the powerless will choose war. But even within politics, the powerless have no reciprocal obligation to act mercifully towards the powerful unless they overpower them. Where that possibility is precluded, as it is for infants, animals, future generations, and so on, it could still be open to their virtual representatives. Might they too be merciless? Is the possibility that they could overpower the present generation of adult human beings one of the possibilities politics allows for? For example: Could a nation-state be taken over by the representatives of the colonized, or by environmental and animal rights activists, or by climate change protestors acting on behalf of people not yet born? Within traditional state theory it is self-evident that the state could not, within the normal course of politics, be taken over by beings from other places, species, or times, or by their representatives. But if the state is just the state of having power over, then that does not hold; there is no such thing as an alien invasion if it takes place within an existing power relationship.

This may seem like a radical conclusion, but it is difficult to avoid if we assume that there is no specifiable limit to the situations in which cruelty should be put first and politics preferred to war. For there to be politics, the powerless must be in a position in which their resistance could be construed as revolt; otherwise there can only be warfare occasionally tempered by mercy rather than politics itself. If that possibility can exist only through virtual representation, then virtual representation is a condition of politics as such. Where there is politics, the powerless must be free to try to overpower the powerful, and if that is impossible, their virtual representatives must be free to do so instead. It might be supposed that a politics of mercy is disempowering and serves only to make active citizens into abject subjects. The opposite is the case. Within the politics of mercy, no one is subject to a power they cannot expect to overpower (or have overpowered on their behalf).

ROBOTIC POLITICS

The human domination of the earth and the future makes these considerations more relevant than ever before, and we may have to adopt a politics of mercy if we want to deal with climate change or any similar long-term environmental threat. The only currently conceivable alternative to human domination would appear to be the domination of superintelligent robots, genetically enhanced humans, or some hybrid of the two. But this only serves to reverse the balance of power and pose the same questions from the other side. One consequence of the argument that politics is nothing but power mercifully exercised was that there is, in theory, nothing to prevent existing states being over-run by their merciless alien subjects. The prospect is not universally viewed with equanimity, nor should it be, because unless these aliens become merciful as they gain power, they will be at war with us, and we will be treated cruelly. The problem with existing political theory is that, because it makes no allowance for the former eventuality, it offers no protection from the latter (cruel treatment by merciless nonhuman overlords).

Let's consider, as a thought experiment, the scenario offered by Nick Bostrom. This assumes the development of a superintelligent singleton, the unique effective decision maker at a global level. A superintelligent AI would be particularly likely to turn into a singleton because it would have an unbounded aggregative utility function, no risk aversion, and maximizing decision rules, and so would have convergent instrumental reasons to acquire control of resources and suppress competition. There is no particular reason to suppose that a successful superintelligence would automatically have other values or goals liable to conflict with or restrain its instrumental values, so it would therefore constitute an overwhelming threat to the independence and indeed survival of the human species.[53]

What would we be looking for from such a singleton? Would we not be putting cruelty first and hoping that in the course of its operations the singleton would not prove to be so indifferent or so sadistic as to kill us or make us submit to unspeakable and (assuming a superintelligence that might be able artificially to prolong our lives or our experiences) protracted physical tortures and emotional cruelties? Given that by the time the superintelligence had become a singleton there would be nothing we could do to deter it or influence its decisions, the focus of our ambitions would be mercy, making the singleton aware of its power, and ensuring that it was never used to the full. So, if there were one virtue that could be programmed into the AI at some earlier stage, it would surely be this—a variant of the first of Asimov's 'three laws of robotics': 'a robot may not injure a human being, or through inaction, allow a human being to come to harm'.[54] Following genetic modification by the superintelligence, we might ourselves no longer be identifiably members of the human species, so we would broaden this to include all those intelligences over whom the superintelligence had power, and specify that the superintelligence should manifest *bonitas*—consistently merciful treatment, even if this went against its instrumental values. At the same time, what limitations would we wish to impose on ourselves, or our virtual representatives, in our dealings with the singleton? None at all.

Relative to a future superintelligent singleton, we are the powerless aliens from another time and species mercilessly supplicating for mercy. But our predicament is in no sense a novel one. This is the position in which humans have generally placed themselves relative to the gods and monsters of tradition, and it is to the merciful exercise of superhuman powers that they have looked to guarantee the survival of their societies. In the early modern period, philosophers like Hobbes and Hume sought to shake off such superstitions to imagine ways in which, through contract or convention, human beings might be said to have rational control of their own destinies, rather than be the powerless subjects of forces beyond their understanding. In retrospect, however, such theories appear to belong to a brief interregnum in which humanity, having freed itself of supernatural powers, had not yet subjected itself irrevocably to powers of its own creation. Rational self-interest itself creates monsters beyond human control, and AI apocalypse is not just a reflection of recent developments in technology, but an extrapolation of a particular set of values, the rational calculation and self-interest identified by Hirschman as the values of capitalism. It is a thought experiment that would be relevant quite independently of the existence of intelligent machines. To be able to overpower the monstrous progeny of our own intelligence has always been the condition of human survival.

Notes

INTRODUCTION

1. Javier Cercas, *Soldiers of Salamis*, tr. Anne McLean (London, 2003), 95–96.
2. This is close to, but does not follow, Ned Markosian, 'Two Puzzles About Mercy', *Philosophical Quarterly* 63 (2013): 269–92. It omits the compassion and moral permissibility requirements and approximates to what he terms the 'normal' rather than the 'flexible' analysis.
3. Jared Diamond, *The World Until Yesterday: What Can We Learn from Traditional Societies* (London, 2012), 5.
4. Justus Lipsius, *Politica*, tr. J. Waszink (Assen, 2004), 325. On Lipsius's relation to the Seneca-Machiavelli debate discussed below in chapter 1, see Christopher Brooke, *Philosophic Pride: Stoicism and Political Thought* (Princeton, 2012), 18–34.
5. *Monita et exempla politica* (Paris, 1605), 110r–19r. See Violet Soen, 'The *Clementia Lipsiana*: Political Analysis, Autobiography and Panegyric', in Erik de

Bom et al., eds., *(Un)masking the Realities of Power* (Leiden, 2011), 207–31.

6. Seneca, 'On Mercy', in *Moral Essays*, tr. J. Basore (Cambridge, MA, 1928), v. 1, 435 (2.3.1) [hereafter *De clem.*].

7. Seneca, *De clem.*, 437 (2.4.3) and 391 (1.11.3).

8. Ibid., 439 (2.5.4) and 443–45 (2.7.1 and 3).

9. Indeed, they positively tripped off the tongue together—e.g., Cicero, *Pro Ligario*, 29; *Ad Herennium*, 2.31.50. See Seneca, *De Ira*, 354 (3.43.5) and *De clem.*, 358 (1.1.4).

10. Ephesians 2.3–5 (NEB).

11. Augustine, *Contra Academicos*, 3.19.42; see Robin Lane Fox, 'Augustine's *Soliloquies* and the Historian', *Studia Patristica* 43 (2006): 185 (cf. Stefan Weinstock, *Divus Iulius* [Oxford, 1971], 237–40.

12. William Shakespeare, *The Merchant of Venice*, 4.1. In *Anger and Forgiveness* (New York, 2016), 206, Martha Nussbaum claims that, in contrast to the 'very different' egalitarian Greco-Roman conception of mercy, Portia's speech exemplifies a 'monarchical conception' of mercy found in the Judeo-Christian tradition in which no 'effort of sympathy or imagination' is required. But in fact, Seneca's model of mercy (the first rounded articulation of the concept in the Greco-Roman world) is explicitly monarchical in conception and opposed to compassion, whereas the Christian one has always been posited on the 'recognition of common humanity' in the incarnation. (See also her ' "If You Could See This Heart":

Mozart's Mercy', in R. R. Caston and R. A. Kaster, eds., *Hope, Joy, and Affection in the Classical World* (Oxford, 2016), 226–40.)

13. K. J. Kesserling, *Mercy and Authority in the Tudor State* (Cambridge, 2003), 56–73. On the earlier period, see Helen Lacey, *The Royal Pardon: Access to Mercy in Fourteenth-Century England* (Woodbridge, 2009), 85–181.

14. Edward Hake, *Epieikeia: A Dialogue on Equity in Three Parts* (New Haven, 1953), 82. Hake offers this as a translation of '*thronus eius fulcitur misericordia*', a variant of the Vulgate's '*Misericordia et veritas custodiunt regem, et roboratur clementia thronus eius*' (Prov. 20.28).

15. *A Circumstantial Account of the Preparations for the Coronation of His Majesty King Charles the Second* (London, 1820), 114.

16. Douglas Hay, 'Property, Authority and the Criminal Law', in Douglas Hay et al., eds., *Albion's Fatal Tree: Crime and Society in Eighteenth-Century England* (New York, 1975), 56 and 48.

17. Montesquieu, *The Spirit of the Laws*, tr. A. M. Cohler et al. (Cambridge, 1989), 92.

18. David Hume, *The History of England* (London, 1834), v. 3, 47; Hume, *Enquiries Concerning Human Understanding* (Oxford, 1975), 308 and 305.

19. Cesare Beccaria, *On Crimes and Punishments*, tr. R. Davies (Cambridge, 1995), 111–12.

20. Gaetano Filangieri, *La scienza della legislazione* (Livorno, 1827), v. 3, 363.

21. Jeremy Bentham, *Works* (London, 1843), v. 1, 520. As Alex Tuckness and John M. Parrish demonstrate in *The Decline of Mercy in Public Life* (Cambridge, 2014), mercy has never subsequently regained its former role. But in recent years there has been a notable uptick in interest amongst legal theorists in the United States; see Austin Sarat and Nasser Hussain, *Forgiveness, Mercy, and Clemency* (Palo Alto, 2006); Austin Sarat, *Mercy on Trial* (Princeton, 2005); and Linda Meyer, *The Justice of Mercy* (Ann Arbor, 2010). This is largely focused on the US justice system and deals with issues somewhat different to those explored in this essay.

22. Albert O. Hirschman, *The Passions and the Interests: Political Arguments for Capitalism before Its Triumph* (Princeton, 1997).

23. Benedict de Spinoza, *Ethics*, tr. E. Curley (London, 1996), 111 (bk 3. II.201/XXXVIII). For Spinoza, *clementia* was not technically a passion (*passio*) but a power (*potentia*), an affect related to the mind not insofar as it acts but ' "insofar as it understands' " (102). See Omero Proietti, ' "Spinoza e il *De Clementia* di Seneca' " *Rivista di storia della filosofia* 63 (2008): 415–35.

24. David Hume, *A Treatise on Human Nature* (Harmondsworth, 1969), 462 and 543–44; Hirschman, *Passions*, 43.

25. Hume, *Enquiries*, 230–31.

26. Spinoza, *Ethics*, 103.

27. Beccaria, *Crimes*, 8; see further Bernard E. Harcourt, *The Illusion of Free Markets: Punishment and the*

Myth of Natural Order (Cambridge, MA, 2011), 53–62.

28. Ibid., 112.

29. Ibid., 8.

CHAPTER I

1. Seneca, *De clem.*, 371 (1.5.2).

2. Recent studies on which this account is based include Melissa Barden Dowling, *Clemency and Cruelty in the Roman World* (Ann Arbor, 2006); Miriam Griffin, 'Clementia after Caesar: From Politics to Philosophy', *Papers of the Langford Latin Seminar*, 11 (2003): 157–82; David Konstan, 'Clemency as a Virtue', *Classical Philology* 100 (2005): 337–46; and Susanna Morton Braund, 'The Anger of Tyrants and the Forgiveness of Kings', in Charles L. Griswold and David Konstan, eds., *Ancient Forgiveness* (Cambridge, 2012), 79–96. For the Greek background, see Jacqueline de Romilly, *La douceur dans la pensée grecque* (Paris, 1979).

3. Cicero, *Selected Orations*, tr. C. D. Yonge (New York, 1875), 241 (*Pro Marc.*, 12).

4. Cicero, *Letters to Atticus*, 8.16.2 (cf. 8.9a.2).

5. Julius Caesar to Oppius and Cornelius Balbus, quoted by Cicero, *Letters*, tr. G. Bell (New York, 1903), 303 (*Ad Att.* 9.7C).

6. Cicero, *Phil.*, 2.116. Cicero oscillated between the two perspectives during Caesar's lifetime before coming down decisively in favour of the latter after his death. Nevertheless it was he who brought the concepts of

clemency and kingship together in the proposal for a Temple of the Clementia Caesaris. See Stefan Weinstock, *Divus Iulius* (Oxford, 1971), 240–41.

7. *De clem.*, 393 (1.12.3).

8. Ibid., 383 (1.9.4–5).

9. Ibid., 391 (1.11.4).

10. Ibid., 365 (1.3.2).

11. See Peter Stacey, *Roman Monarchy and the Renaissance Prince* (Cambridge, 2007).

12. *De clem.*, 393–95 (1.12.4).

13. Niccolò Machiavelli, *The Prince*, tr. G. Bull (London, 1999), 54 (ch. 17).

14. Ibid., 24 and 53.

15. Ibid., 50.

16. Ibid., 57.

17. That's the difference between monarchies and republics, as he explains in the *Discourses*, 2.2.

18. *De clem.*, 377 (1.7.3); Machiavelli, *Prince*, 80.

19. Ibid., 49.

20. Hirschman, *Passions and the Interests*, 33.

21. The argument here follows David Quint, *Montaigne and the Quality of Mercy* (Princeton, 1998) against David Lewis Schaefer, *The Political Philosophy of Montaigne* (Ithaca, 1990).

22. Michel de Montaigne, *The Complete Essays*, tr. M. A. Screech (London, 1991), 500–1 (2.12).

23. Ibid., 679 and 669 (2.12).

24. Ibid., 672 and 617 (2.12).

25. Ibid., 59 (1.14).

26. Ibid., 480–81 and 485 (2.11).

27. Ibid., 1045 (3.8).
28. Ibid., 737 (2.17).
29. Ibid., 901 and 906 (3.1). See Robert J. Collins, 'Montaigne's Rejection of Reason of State in "*De l'utile et de l'honneste*"', *Sixteenth Century Journal* 23 (1992): 71–94.
30. Montaigne, *Complete Essays*, 140–49 (1.24).
31. Ibid., 904–5 (3.1).
32. Ibid., 1205 (3.12).
33. Judith N. Shklar, 'Putting Cruelty First', *Daedalus* 111 (3) (1982): 17–27, expanded in *Ordinary Vices* (Cambridge, MA, 1984), 7–44, and 'The Liberalism of Fear', in Nancy Rosenblum, ed., *Liberalism and the Moral Life* (Cambridge, MA, 1989), 21–38.
34. Shklar, 'Putting', 17, and 'Liberalism', 29.
35. Shklar, 'Liberalism', 27.
36. Shklar, 'Putting', 25, quoting Montaigne, 'On Vanity'.
37. Ibid., 17, and *Ordinary Vices*, 8.
38. Ibid., 18.
39. Shklar, 'Liberalism', 23.
40. Ibid., 30.
41. Ibid., 27.
42. Ibid., 26–27.
43. Ibid., 37.
44. Ibid., 37; see also John Kekes, 'Cruelty and Liberalism', *Ethics* 106 (1996): 834–44.
45. Ibid., 35.
46. See Katrina Forrester, 'Judith Shklar, Bernard Williams and Political Realism', *European Journal of*

Political Theory 11 (2012): 247–72, who notes, in particular, their diverging responses to Rawls.

47. Bernard Williams, *In the Beginning Was the Deed* (Princeton, 2005), 59 [hereafter IBD]. See further Matt Sleat, *Liberal Realism* (Manchester, 2013), esp. 112–31, and Paul Sagar, 'From Scepticism to Liberalism? Bernard Williams, the Foundations of Liberalism and Political Realism', *Political Studies* 64 (2014): 368–84.

48. Ibid., 1–2.

49. Ibid., 47.

50. Ibid., 50.

51. Ibid., 49.

52. Ibid., 3.

53. Ibid., 4. See Edward Hall, 'Bernard Williams and the Basic Legitimation Demand: A Defence', *Political Studies* 63 (June 2015): 466–80.

54. Ibid., 5–6.

55. Ibid., 11.

56. Ibid., 89 and 6.

57. Ibid., 5.

58. Ibid., 10.

59. Ibid., 6.

60. Ibid., 5–6.

61. Bernard Williams, *Truth and Truthfulness* (Princeton, 2002), 228–29. On the limitations of Williams's account, see Janosch Prinz and Enzo Rossi, 'Political Realism as Ideology Critique', *Critical Review of International Social and Political Philosophy* 20 (2017): 348–65.

62. Quoted in Theresa Urbainczyk, *Slave Revolts in Antiquity* (Abingdon, 2014), 52.

63. Ibid., 135.

64. Cf. *De clem.*, 405 (1.16.1–4).

65. Ibid., 407–9 (1.18.1–3).

66. Seneca, *Letters,* tr. R. M. Gummere (New York, 2016), 106 (*Ep.* xlvii.11).

67. Ibid.

68. *De clem.*, 425 (1.26.1).

69. Ibid., 413 (1.19.8, cf.1.1.5 and 2.1.1 and Cicero, *Pro Lig.*, 37).

70. IBD, 9.

71. Bernard Williams, *Ethics and the Limits of Philosophy* (London, 1985), 27.

72. Ibid., 30.

73. IBD, 4–6.

74. Ibid., 59.

75. See F. S. Naiden, *Ancient Supplication* (Oxford, 2006).

76. See Ivan Nagel, *Autonomy and Mercy: Reflections on Mozart's Operas* (Cambridge, MA, 1991), 49–50.

77. For an alternative genealogy, see Thom Brooks, 'Bernard Williams, Republicanism, and the Liberalism of Fear', in A. Perry and C. Herrera, eds., *The Moral Philosophy of Bernard Williams* (Newcastle, 2013), 109–13.

78. *De clem.*, 393 (1.12.3).

79. IBD, 59. For a more optimistic assessment of what Machiavelli might contribute to a liberalism of fear, see Thomas Osborne, 'Machiavelli and the Liberalism

of Fear', *History of the Human Sciences* 30:5 (2017): 68–85.

80. *Prince*, 47 (ch. 14).

CHAPTER 2

1. On the lack of a theory of sovereignty in Hume, see Paul Sagar, *The Opinion of Mankind: Sociability and the Theory of the State from Hobbes to Smith* (Princeton, 2018), 103–38.

2. Hanna Pitkin, *Wittgenstein and Justice* (Berkeley, 1972), 276–79.

3. See Steven Lukes, *Power: A Radical View* (London, 2004).

4. Martha Albertson Fineman, 'The Vulnerable Subject: Anchoring Equality in the Human Condition', *Yale Journal of Law and Feminism* 20:1 (2008): 2.

5. Robert E. Goodin, *Protecting the Vulnerable* (Chicago, 1985), 112.

6. See Martha C. Nussbaum, *Women and Human Development: The Capabilities Approach* (Cambridge, 2000), and Catriona Mackenzie, 'The Importance of Relational Autonomy and Capabilities for an Ethics of Vulnerability', in Catriona Mackenzie, Wendy Rogers, and Susan Dodds, eds., *Vulnerability: New Essays in Ethics and Feminist Philosophy* (Oxford, 2013), 33–59.

7. Hume, *Enquiries*, 190.

8. Hume, *Essays*, 413, 203, and 274, and *Treatise*, 630. See further Ryan Hanley, 'David Hume and the "Politics of Humanity"', *Political Theory* 39 (2011):

205–33, and Remy Debes, 'Humanity, Sympathy and the Puzzle of Hume's Second Enquiry', *British Journal for the History of Philosophy* 15 (2007): 27–57.

9. With regard to slaves, Adam Smith attributed to 'gentle usage' the same benefits that Seneca attributed to mercy: 'Gentle usage renders the slave not only more faithful, but more intelligent, and, therefore, upon a double account, more useful. He approaches more to the condition of a free servant' (*Wealth of Nations* [London, 1776], v. 2, 186).

10. Hume, *Enquiries*, 191.

11. Hume, *Treatise*, 539 and 547.

12. Hume, *Enquiries*, 181–90.

13. John Rawls, *A Theory of Justice* (Oxford, 1971), 126–27. On the differences between Hume and Rawls, see Andrew Lister, 'Hume and Rawls on the Circumstances and Priority of Justice', *History of Political Thought* 36 (2005): 664–95.

14. Ibid., 127–28.

15. See Brian Barry, *Theories of Justice* (Hemel Hempstead, 1986); Michael Sandel, *Liberalism and the Limits of Justice* (Cambridge, 1998); Martha Nussbaum, *Frontiers of Justice* (Cambridge, MA, 2006); and G. A. Cohen, *Rescuing Justice and Equality* (Cambridge, MA, 2008). For a defence, see Simon Hope, 'The Circumstances of Justice', *Hume Studies* 36 (2010): 125–48.

16. Rawls describes (1) as 'a cooperative venture for mutual advantage' (*Theory of Justice*, 126), and (3) as 'a scheme of cooperation for reciprocal advantage' (33, cf. 14). (2), which serves to justify the transition

from (1) to (3), is no different: it involves 'rational persons concerned to further their own interests' who 'choose together, in one joint act' principles that reflect 'the symmetry of everyone's relations to each other' (11–12). Rawls later seeks to distinguish reciprocity from mutual advantage in *Political Liberalism* (New York, 2011), 17; see further Jiwei Ci, *Two Faces of Justice* (Cambridge, MA, 2006), 135–56.

17. See Fineman, 'Vulnerable Subject', and Eva Feder Kittay, 'Human Dependency and Rawlsian Equality', in Diana T. Myers, ed., *Feminists Rethink the Self* (Boulder, 1997), 219–66.

18. The circumstances of mercy are thus also very different from what Michael Sandel calls the 'circumstances of benevolence' (*Liberalism and the Limits of Justice*, 32–33).

19. Rawls, *Theory of Justice*, 511.

20. Amartya Sen, *The Idea of Justice* (London, 2009).

21. Adam Smith quoted in Sen, 128.

22. Ibid., vii.

23. Ibid., 389.

24. Ibid., vii.

25. Judith Shklar, *Faces of Injustice* (New Haven, 1990).

26. Martha Nussbaum notes the potential affinity between Adam Smith's impartial spectatorship and mercy in 'Equity and Mercy', *Philosophy & Public Affairs* 22 (1993): 110. See further ch. 3 below.

27. Hume, *Treatise,* 536, 549, 541. See further Michael L. Frazer, *The Enlightenment of Sympathy* (Oxford, 2010), 66–88.

28. Ibid., 541–42.

29. Ibid., 551.

30. Ibid., 630.

31. Hume, *Enquiries*, 305.

32. Ibid., 306.

33. Hume, *Treatise*, 550.

34. See further Sagar, *The Opinion of Mankind*, 49–54.

35. Hume, *Enquiries*, 190.

36. David K. Lewis, *Convention* (Cambridge, MA, 1969), 3–4, 5–6.

37. Donald Davidson, 'Radical Interpretation', in *Inquiries into Truth and Interpretation* (Oxford, 2001), 137.

38. Donald Davidson, 'Truth and Thought', in *Inquiries into Truth and Interpretation*, 168–69.

39. Donald Davidson, 'The Method of Truth in Metaphysics', in *Inquiries into Truth and Interpretation,* 200.

40. Hume, *Enquiries*, 305.

41. Donald Davidson, 'Communication and Convention', in *Inquiries into Truth and Interpretation*, 279.

42. Donald Davidson, 'A Nice Derangement of Epitaphs', in *The Essential Davidson* (Oxford, 2006), 251–65.

43. Ibid., 265.

44. Rawls, *Theory of Justice*, 3.

CHAPTER 3

1. Thomas Aquinas, *Summa theologiae*, 1a.21.4

2. Anselm of Canterbury, *Major Works* (Oxford, 1998), 91–94 (*Proslogion*, 9–12).

3. Jeffrie Murphy, 'Mercy and Legal Justice', in Jeffrie Murphy and Jean Hampton, *Forgiveness and Mercy* (Cambridge, 1988), 167, 169, 172.

4. Ibid., 176–77.

5. H. Scott Hestevold, 'Disjunctive Desert', *American Philosophical Quarterly* 20 (1983): 357–63, and 'Justice to Mercy', *Philosophy and Phenomenological Research* 46 (1985): 281–91.

6. Markosian, 'Two Puzzles', 277.

7. See George Rainbolt, 'Mercy: An Independent Imperfect Virtue', *American Philosophical Quarterly* 27 (1990): 169–73.

8. John Tasioulas, 'Mercy', *Proceedings of the Aristotelian Society* 103 (2003): 119.

9. Aristotle, *Nicomachean Ethics*, tr. J.A.K. Thompson (Harmondsworth, 1976), 173 (1129b17–20).

10. Ibid., 199–200 (1137a31–1138a4).

11. Aristotle, *Rhetoric*, tr. W. D. Ross (New York, 2010), 50 (1374b).

12. Martha C. Nussbaum, 'Equity and Mercy', *Philosophy & Public Affairs* 22 (1993): 87, 90, 105.

13. John Tasioulas, 'The Paradox of Equity', *Cambridge Law Journal* 55 (1996): 458–59.

14. Tasioulas, 'Mercy', 113.

15. Martha C. Nussbaum, *Love's Knowledge* (New York, 1992), 99–100.

16. Nussbaum, 'Equity', 93n19.

17. Ibid., 96.

18. Martha C. Nussbaum, *Frontiers of Justice: Disability, Nationality, Species Membership* (Cambridge, MA, 2006), 47, 22, 24–25 (cf. 63).

19. Ibid., 92 and 409.

20. Clarence Gallagher, *Canon Law and the Christian Community* (Rome, 1978), 136 ('*aequitas est iustitia dulcore misericordiae temperata*').

21. Wolsey quoted in Stuart E. Prall, 'The Development of Equity in Tudor England', *American Journal of Legal History* 8 (1964): 7.

22. John Goodwin defended Colonel Pride's Purge of Parliament on the basis of 'that virtue which the Grecians call *epieikeia*, we Equitie, which rectifies, limits, and restrains the law'. Quoted in Mark Fortier, *The Culture of Equity in Early Modern England* (Aldershot, 2005), 168.

23. Andrew Sharp, ed., *Political Ideas of the English Civil Wars* (London, 1983), 172.

24. Richard Overton, *Works* (Bristol, 2003), 238.

25. Gerrard Winstanley, *The Complete Works* (Oxford, 2009), v. 2, 140 and 92; v. 1, 499ff.

26. Ibid., v. 1, 506–7.

27. Romans 11.32.

28. Augustine quoted in Ilaria Ramelli, *The Christian Doctrine of Apokatastasis* (Leiden, 2013), 664.

29. Unlike those who maintain that 'some are elected to salvation, and others are reprobated', Winstanley argues that the Saviour 'comes not to destroy any but to save all' (*Works*, v. 2, 136).

30. John Selden, *Table Talk* (London, 1689), 43.

31. Murphy, 'Mercy', 181 and 183.

32. George Rainbolt, 'Mercy: In Defense of Caprice', *Noûs* 31 (1997): 226–41.

33. Anselm, *Works*, 91.

34. Ross Harrison, 'The Equality of Mercy', in H. Gross and R. Harrison, eds., *Jurisprudence* (Oxford, 1992), 118.

35. IBD, 62.

36. Raymond Geuss, *Philosophy and Real Politics* (Princeton, 2008), 70–71.

37. Friedrich Nietzsche, *Human, All Too Human*, tr. R. J. Hollingdale (Cambridge, 1996), 318–19 (WS, 34), and *On the Genealogy of Morals*, tr. D. Smith (Oxford, 1996), 53–54 (2.10).

38. Friedrich Nietzsche, *Beyond Good and Evil*, tr. W. Kaufmann (New York, 1966), 114 (201).

39. Judith Shklar, *Ordinary Vices* (Cambridge, MA, 1984), 7; see also her *Faces of Injustice* (New Haven, 1990).

40. Philippa Foot, *Natural Goodness* (Oxford, 2001), 78.

41. See Simon Kirchin, ed., *Thick Concepts* (Oxford, 2013).

42. Williams, *Ethics*, 144 (cf. 155ff).

43. Hilary Putnam, *The Collapse of the Fact/Value Dichotomy* (Cambridge, MA, 2002), 34–35.

44. Williams, *Ethics*, 185.

45. Samuel Scheffler, 'Morality Through Thick and Thin', *Philosophical Review* 96 (1987): 411–34.

46. IBD, 47.

47. Nietzsche, *Genealogy*, 56 (2.11). In his account justice, too, was originally a thick concept, a form of exchange between equals that continued to exist only 'for so long as the power of those who have concluded these compacts remain equal or similar' (*Human*, 314 [WS, 26]).

48. IBD, 48. On Williams and Nietzsche, see Maude-marie Clark, 'On the Rejection of Morality: Bernard Williams's Debt to Nietzsche', in R. Schacht, ed., *Nietzsche's Postmoralism* (Cambridge, 2001), 100–22, and Raymond Geuss, *Outside Ethics* (Princeton, 2005), 219–33.

49. Putnam, *Collapse*, 62–63.

50. Adam Smith, *The Theory of Moral Sentiments* (Oxford, 1976), 21 (1.i.4.6). Fonna Forman-Barzilai compares Smith's response to cruelty to that of Shklar in *Adam Smith and the Circles of Sympathy* (Cambridge, 2010), 234–37.

51. Nussbaum, 'Equity', 110.

52. IBD, 2.

53. Ibid., 8 and 11.

54. Nietzsche, *Genealogy*, 12 (1.2); Nietzsche, *Beyond*, 158 (229), and 202 (258).

CHAPTER 4

1. Quentin Skinner, *Visions of Politics* (Cambridge, 2002), v. 2, 369, 378, 386, 404, 407n236; see also *From Humanism to Hobbes* (Cambridge, 2018), 341–83.

2. Thomas Hobbes, *The Elements of Law Natural and Politic* (Oxford, 1994), 124–25.

3. Thomas Hobbes, *Leviathan* (Cambridge, 1991), 121. See further David Runciman, 'The Concept of the State: The Sovereignty of a Fiction', in Quentin Skinner and Bo Stråth, eds., *States and Citizens* (Cambridge, 2003), 28–38.

4. Thomas Hobbes, *On the Citizen*, tr. M. Silverthorne (Cambridge, 1998), 76 [translation modified].

5. Hobbes, *Leviathan*, 87.

6. Ibid., 106; Hobbes, *De Cive* (Oxford, 1983), 121 and 124. The first English translation of *De Cive* translates *misericordia* as 'mercy', whereas Silverthorne opts, oddly, for 'pity'.

7. Hobbes, *On the Citizen*, 30–31 (cf. *Elements*, 80–81).

8. Hobbes, *Leviathan*, 121 (88). See further Charles D. Tarlton, ' "To Avoyd the Present Stroke of Death": Despotical Dominion, Force, and Legitimacy in Hobbes's *Leviathan*', *Philosophy* 74 (1999): 221–45.

9. Hobbes, *Elements*, 108.

10. Hobbes, *On the Citizen*, 102.

11. Hobbes, *Leviathan*, 138 and 142.

12. Ibid., 141.

13. Ibid., 106.

14. Hobbes, *Elements*, 80 (cf. *On the Citizen*, 29–30), and *Leviathan*, 88–89.

15. If it were true, then the concept of being 'sufficiently known' (or having a 'known disposition' in the *Leviathan*) would be superfluous.

16. Hobbes, *Leviathan*, 118–19.

17. Ibid., 248 and 106. Compleasance is all but ignored in the vast literature on Hobbes, but see Rosamond Rhodes, 'Hobbes's Fifth Law of Nature and its Implications', *Hobbes Studies* 22 (2009): 144–59, and for the background, Teresa Bejan, *Mere Civility* (Cambridge, MA, 2017).

18. Hobbes, *Elements,* 91. In *On the Citizen* this law is said to require that people be considerate (*commodus*) to others (48).

19. See Eustache de Refuge, whose work appeared in English as *The Art of Complaisance, or the Means to Oblige in Conversation* (London, 1673). On Hobbes's interest in this literature, see Skinner, *From Humanism,* 162–89.

20. Joseph Addison, *Works* (London, 1721), v. 4, 273; Hobbes, *Leviathan,* 106 and 119.

21. Ibid., 106.

22. 'As nature has given man the superiority above woman, by endowing him with greater strength both of mind and body; it is his part to alleviate that superiority, as much as possible ... by civility, by respect, by complaisance, and, in a word, by gallantry'. David Hume, *Essays* (Indianapolis, 1985), 133.

23. Hobbes, *Leviathan,* 106.

24. Hobbes, *On the Citizen,* 69–70 .

25. IBD, 3.

26. Derek Parfit, *Reasons and Persons* (Oxford, 1984) 209–17, picks up Hume's comparison of the soul to 'a republic, or commonwealth' and interprets it (somewhat anachronistically) as a nation. However, a nation cannot be reduced to 'citizens acting in various ways on its territory' (471–72), for concepts like 'citizen' and 'territory' assume nationhood.

27. Max Weber, *From Max Weber: Essays in Sociology,* tr. H. Gerth and C. Wright Mills (London, 1991), 78.

28. IBD, 62.

29. John Searle, *The Construction of Social Reality* (London, 1995), 36.

30. Parfit, *Reasons*, 210. This is perhaps the implication of what Raymond Geuss terms 'philosophical anarchism' in *History and Illusion in Politics* (Cambridge, 2001), 53.

31. Ibid., 213–14.

32. Thomas Hobbes, *Seven Philosophical Problems* (London, 1682), sig. A2v.

33. Charles Tilly, 'War Making and State Making as Organized Crime', in Peter Evans, Dietrich Rueschemeyer, and Theda Skocpol, eds., *Bringing the State Back In* (Cambridge, 1985), 169–87.

34. Bernard Williams, *Moral Luck* (Cambridge, 1981), 20–39. See also Christopher Kutz, 'Against Political Luck', in Daniel Callcut, ed., *Reading Bernard Williams* (London, 2009), 242–61. For a discussion of moral luck in relation to forgiveness, see Charles L. Griswold, *Forgiveness: A Philosophical Exploration* (New York, 2007), 130–33.

35. To use Nagel's own example, *Mortal Questions* (Cambridge, 1979), 30: 'If the Decembrists had succeeded in overthrowing Nicholas 1 in 1825 and establishing a constitutional regime, they would be heroes'. But they didn't and were not.

36. This leaves little scope for an alignment with republicanism of the kind envisaged by Philip Pettit in 'Political Realism Meets Civic Republicanism', *Critical Review of International Social and Political Philosophy* 20 (2017): 331–47.

37. See Axel Gosseries, 'Three Models of Intergenerational Reciprocity', in A. Gosseries and L. H. Meyer, eds., *Intergenerational Justice* (Oxford, 2009), 119–46.

38. Edmund Burke, *Reflections on the Revolution in France* (Oxford, 1993), 96.

39. See Brian Barry, 'Justice as Reciprocity', in *Democracy, Power and Justice: Essays in Political Theory* (Oxford, 1989), 463–94.

40. Andrea Sangiovanni, 'Global Justice, Reciprocity, and the State', *Philosophy & Public Affairs* 35 (2007): 3–39.

41. Hobbes, *Leviathan*, 141. See further Mary Nyquist, *Arbitrary Rule: Slavery, Tyranny, and the Power of Life and Death* (Chicago, 2013), 293–325.

42. James C. Scott, *Weapons of the Weak: Everyday Forms of Peasant Resistance* (New Haven, 1985), 136.

43. For one possible example, see Karuna Mantena, 'Another Realism: The Politics of Gandhian Non-violence', *American Political Science Review* 106 (2012): 455–70.

44. Hume, *Enquiries*, 191.

45. IBD, 6.

46. Hobbes, *Leviathan*, 180.

47. Tom Paine, *Rights of Man* (Oxford, 1995), 92.

48. Alexander Herzen, *From the Other Shore*, tr. M. Budberg (London, 1957), 37. On the 'tyranny of the contemporary', see Stephen M. Gardner, *A Perfect Moral Storm: The Ethical Tragedy of Climate Change* (New York, 2011), 143–84.

49. Edmund Burke, *The Writings and Speeches of Edmund Burke* (New York, 1992), v. 9, 629.

50. See Anja Karnein, 'Can We Represent Future Gener-
    ations?' in Iñigo González-Ricoy and Axel Gosseries,
    eds., *Institutions for Future Generations* (Oxford,
    2016), 83–97, and Jane Mansbridge, 'Rethinking
    Representation', *American Political Science Review* 97
    (2003): 515–28.

51. On vanguardism and vulnerability, see also Lea Ypi,
    'Politically Constructed Solidarity: The Idea of a
    Cosmopolitan Avant-Garde', *Contemporary Political
    Theory* 9 (2010): 120–30.

52. Georg Lukács, *Lenin: A Study on the Unity of His
    Thought*, tr. N. Jacobs (London, 2009), 34.

53. Nick Bostrom, *Superintelligence: Paths, Dangers,
    Strategies* (Oxford, 2014).

54. Ibid., 170 (first formulated in Isaac Asimov's short
    story 'Runaround' [1942]).

Index